Book #1 in the Light Up Your Life Series

Joy-Full Seasoned Women

A Guide to Bearing Fruit and Radiating Joy in Your Second Half of Life

CHRISTINE BOERSMA SMITH

Radiant Joy

Butterfly Books Publishing

Special Ordering Information:

Quantity sales. Special discounts are available on quantity purchases by churches, parishes, women's groups, associations, and others. For details, contact the "Special Sales Department" at the address above or through RadiantJoy.us.

Would you like to gain more depth and experience more fullness of joy as you read and beyond this book?

 As my way of saying, "Thank you!" for reading *Joy-Full Seasoned Women,* I'd like to give you a special Bonus Gift Package that goes with this book.

It includes:

The *Joy-Full Seasoned Women Workbook.* For individual use and especially recommended for those wanting to work through this book with a group, this workbook will help you go even deeper, reflect after each chapter, and have space to write your thoughts in a place you can refer back to. The downloadable and printable e-book is available with the Bonus Package online, or you can purchase a printed version to be mailed to your doorstep.

- ○ *Please see the copyright page for ordering instructions for groups interested in buying multiple books at a discount.*
- ○ *I also offer an 8-week online Joy-Full Seasoned Women Workshop that I will lead for those wishing to go through the book with a group of seasoned Christian women, as led by the author.*

The 21-Day Joy Challenge. So often, it's easy to read something but then struggle to live it out. By joining the 21-Day Joy Challenge offered to readers, you can encourage yourself to live joyfully. For 21 days, you will receive a daily challenge email, and on the final day, you will receive a gift set of pretty printable cards, each with an inspiring quote and an activity to promote joy.

Eleven Spiritual Principles. A free PDF download to show you the spiritual principles I have learned and live by.

Fruitful Prayer. A free PDF download to guide you in your prayer life.

The Radiant Joy Challenge: 21 Days to More Joy, Greater Peace, and New Intimacy with God Devotional Book. This devotional-style challenge book is more comprehensive than the email challenge and incorporates daily prayers and journal prompts.

Download this Bonus Package at:
radiantjoy.us/joy-book.

Praise for *Joy-Full Seasoned Women*:

"As I finished reading the last page of this book, weeping with joy, I was reminded of when my husband and I were dating, and he said, 'You're a Keeper!' Well, this book is a 'Keeper' -- one that I will treasure all of my days! So many aspects of the book will be a continued source of joy and encouragement for years to come, not only through re-reading the book but by staying connected with Christine. I tried to end my life at age eleven and committed myself to a mental hospital in my forties because of my despair about not hearing from God like my grandfather said he did. Thankfully, at age 78, I am thankful to commune with God continually, and this book will be a valuable asset in my walk. Thank you, dear Christine, for your faithfulness and perseverance. May God bless all your remaining days on this earth.

Barbara Hemphill
www.BarbaraHemphill.com
www.ProductiveEnvironment.com
"Accomplish Your Work & Enjoy Your Life, Increase Productivity & Profitability, and Leave a Legacy that Matters!"

Contents

Preface

When I entered the second half of my life, I found myself pondering my life's mission. Twelve years ago, the Holy Spirit revealed it to me through a prophecy that seemed well-suited. Accordingly, I began serving in a Spirit-led ministry that facilitates forgiveness, healing, and spiritual freedom.

I've had the humbling privilege of listening to countless women recap their difficult life stories, leading them through prayer sessions with compassion, and then guiding them into emotional release and spiritual transformation. The Lord brings them healing from woundedness and painful memories, and sometimes healing of physical infirmities.

In each case, with the Holy Spirit as the true leader of the prayer sessions, women have uncovered limiting or deceptive beliefs that were lies, feelings of being stuck, identity issues, hurts, abuse, word curses, and more—most of which had originated from decades-old events. Through these sessions, the majority are set free of disruptive lies, old grudges, destructive memories, and spiritual oppression. Others are grateful for receiving love and compassion and at least obtain significant relief and peace.

My experience has shown me that many women have chronic issues that need to be addressed and can be healed with help. I have needed that myself and the difference that healing and spiritual cleansing (a.k.a. deliverance) have made in my life is like night versus day, lifting me from darkness into the Light!

Those women, my journey, my relationship with God, and my passion for joy have inspired me to write this book, which Jesus and the Holy Spirit have given me as my current assignment in the Kingdom. And I am thrilled to say, "Yes, Lord, Thy will be done, so help me, God!"

My writing is primarily about Jesus, the Holy Spirit, and You. I am enthusiastic about joy, and I want to share my Joy-Full ideas with everyone God nudges to desire more joy, especially for seasoned Catholics and other Christian women. By "seasoned," I include those born before 1970 or ladies in whatever they consider their second half of life. I've also heard younger women express the desire to read this guide to experience more joy now and prepare themselves for what's ahead.

Welcome!

Introduction

My husband and I don't think of ourselves as elders.

Our daughter is blessed with a beautiful gift of hospitality, and she and her husband frequently host large parties in their backyard, always including parents and children. We are pleased to be invited to their gatherings, sometimes pitching in and assisting with food prep or organizing games.

At a recent birthday party for our granddaughter turning three, we had no assigned tasks and were simply guests. We left feeling old! The parents attending were young and attentive to their children and the other little guests' parents. Although they politely said "Hello" to us and replied when we started conversations, they quickly moved on to speak with the younger crowd, and we understood. Honestly, we weren't engaging. I held back because I couldn't recall which parent came with which partner or child. I was out of my usual Christian milieu. The conversations we started were banal.

These recent interactions differed significantly from those at birthday parties for our grandson, who's now twenty. The last birthday party of his that we went to was in 2010. The difference, it seemed to us, was that we are a decade and a half older now than we were in his preschool years. We often find ourselves shocked to be the oldest in a group, mainly because we are both still very active—my husband in his career and I in writing and ministry.

Our culture typically uses the first quarter of life to prepare young people for the second quarter as they acquire social skills, education, and ideas about their future. We probably all tried to prepare our kids well. Then, when the children leave home, our work life may shift or end, and we might realize that we have entered a new season of life for which we are unprepared. Many of us find ourselves blessed, yet we also face unexpected challenges and maybe a loss of identity if we allow our roles to define us.

I know this only too well! In the first half of my life, I was a perfectionist striving to do everything right. I became a grandmother at fifty-five while we still had two teenagers. I'd found my identity in my roles and my work. When my roles changed, I floundered, exploring creativity, making new friends and acquaintances through shared activities, undertaking home improvement and organizing projects, and keeping myself busy while my husband was traveling for work. I didn't slow down and rest. I didn't embrace peace, tranquility, and joy.

The kids sailed away from home, leaving complications in their wake. My family of origin was scattered across the country in five states, with my closest sibling a fifteen-hour drive away. I yearned for meaningful relationships with God and other Christians, particularly women near my age who share the desire to follow Jesus and be led by the Spirit, to grow spiritually, and to live fruitful and fulfilling lives with love, peace, and joy.

Thanks be to the Father, Son, and Holy Spirit, who have significantly transformed me. I feel called to help others enjoy blessed intimacy with God, know each person of the Trinity through personal encounters and regular two-way conversations, seek God's input when making choices, and tap into the joy that Jesus came to give us. Joy strengthens us, and He wants to make our joy complete as we remain in His abiding love.

Now, let's look at Jesus!

Jesus was a radical. He was bold and outspoken. He was unafraid of the religious authorities of His day. He was God and a man of contemplative prayer and mighty, astounding, miraculous teaching, preaching, and action. Jesus spent daily time alone with the Father, checking in throughout His days and taking directions from the Father.

He was a healer. He drove out demons who knew He was the Messiah and cowered before Him. He was generous. He was compassionate and merciful. He had righteous anger when the situation warranted it. He spoke truth to power. John 14:6 says Jesus is the Way, the Truth, and the Life.

Jesus modeled the Way Himself. Imitating Jesus is a very high standard, but we have many illustrative lessons in Scripture and a handful of basics to embrace. Let us pray that we can truly live according to Jesus' ways. Some excellent authorities suggest this is what it takes to get into heaven. "The Way" implies a journey to a destination. In Christianity, that destination is Eternal Life.

Even though Jesus set a very high standard, His unambiguous Word establishes that we should embrace Him as our model, follow in His footsteps, and imitate Him and His love. After washing His disciples' feet, Jesus said, "I have given you an example. Do as I have done to you" (John 13:25, NLT).

I must admit that I have fallen extremely short of imitating Christ, especially when I didn't realize that was my mandate. I spent the first half of my life attached to other people's favorable, "successful" judgment. I wish I could say I'm all done with that, that I never need external validation to feel "good enough," let alone valuable. Most of the time, I feel healed, blessed, and grateful. But when I slip backward, the rusty lies Satan tries to put in my head are:

1. Love must be earned (or I must earn love); and
2. Perfection is possible.

Although I sometimes feels a twinge of hurt or offense and forget the truth, I have come to believe the truth:

1. Love is a free gift, and
2. Human perfection is impossible.

Joy is a fruit of the Holy Spirit that repeatedly occurs in both the Old and New Testaments, even in Jesus' discourses. As I talk about how to let joy light up your life, the importance and availability of hearing from God emerges. This is not a book on all the ways believers can pray. I write of prayer methods that enkindle hearing the "voice" of God, whether that is through Scripture, the "still small voice within" like Elijah experienced, or a prompting from the Holy Spirit. "Hearing" may also come from a meditation, song lyrics, or something unexpected that seems to be a "God thing."

So, let me describe the way I begin my days—in what I call my Quiet Time—which, depending on the day, may precede or follow attending Mass and other forms of prayer and worship.

At home in a tiny and remote California coastal town, I created a joy-inspired prayer corner separate from the bedroom and the common areas of the house. Its comfortable armchair is upholstered with whimsical, eight-inch, teal frogs that make me smile, a footrest, good lighting, and a side table for my Bible, journal, pens, highlighter, a handkerchief, and tea. With my dog beside me, I begin by reading and pondering a short entry from a daily devotional, noting any questions or insights in my journal. My routine isn't exactly the same every day because the Holy Spirit often prompts me with what's next. If I am currently praying a nine-day series—such as the Surrender Novena or (especially pre-Pentecost) a Novena to the Holy Spirit—I will usually pray that next, again pondering and journaling insights or anything I feel God is revealing to me.

In recent months, I have written in my journal the question I'd most like God to answer, if He so wills. It might be about my writing, health, family, what to focus on that day, or something else. On my iPhone (in Airplane mode), I play a guided meditation that opens with visualizing myself with Jesus, set against instrumental music or nature sounds for a soft background as I present my pre-written question to Jesus and "listen" for His response.

Answers typically come to me in spontaneous thoughts that I journal. If I'm unsure whether the thought was from the Lord, myself, or the adversary, I ask the Holy Spirit and usually receive clarification. Time flies by; I thank Jesus and re-read what I wrote. Sometimes, what I wrote sends me to Scripture.

Next, I open my phone's Hallow app to the daily gospel or another passage and use *Lectio Divina* (an approach described in Chapter 6). I often choose among other offerings on the app, such as concise inspirational words from Father Mike Schmitz or Father Dave Pivonka. I offer petitions and gratitude. Before I start the rest of the day, I like to go outside, stand on the earth in bare feet, bend down to touch the ground, and then reach toward the heavens, praising God in gesture, words, and song.

What does this Quiet Time do for me? It centers me. It means I am obediently and wisely seeking the Kingdom of God and His righteousness first, believing (hopefully, every day) that Jesus will take care of whatever might otherwise hijack my thoughts away from godly thoughts or make me anxious or afraid. True surrender eliminates concerns.

I recently learned that "trying" to surrender means you're not surrendering. Do this, please. Pick up a cup of water. Now, try to drop it—keep trying! You can't keep trying if you've already let it go. The bottom line is, don't just try to surrender. Do it! Chapter 3 discusses how.

Actual surrender increases trust in God and confidence that God is *for* you and *with* you, encouraging a lifestyle of surrender and reliance on God.

From a practical point of view, my Quiet Time sets my priorities for the day ahead and afterward. It clears out negativity and clarifies what matters most and how I'm urged to spend the day. From a higher perspective, I have gained a greater understanding of my identity in Christ, which helps me become a more available disciple.

So, let's jump in and explore truly "abiding" with God, which makes our joy complete. And let's be our REAL selves! When I refer to the REAL you, I mean "genuine," exactly what you appear to be, without artificiality, insecurity, pretensions, or ostentation. The REAL you is fair, honest, firmly established, original, and natural. The REAL self is also someone who's been set FREE. More on this is also in Chapter 3.

Let's invite the Holy Spirit to empower us as we walk with Him and enjoy His gifts, fruit, truth, and understanding. Let's align with Jesus, like the servants at the wedding at Cana, listening to Him and doing "whatever he tells us to do" (see John 2:5). Let's open our hearts, minds, and spiritual eyes and ears, and experience the joy of the Lord in the abundance Jesus wants for us. Let's allow ourselves to be held in our Father's heart and loving arms and enjoy fellowship with our brothers and sisters in Christ.

Prayer

Jesus, please grant that I may know You well and follow You, walking the path of trust and surrender. Give me a profound spirit of faith so I recognize Your voice and the Father's will. Please, Lord, with Your outpouring of grace, would You help me make You the Lord who directs my free will, conforming me to what You ask of me, whatever the circumstances?

Holy Spirit, would You empower me to transform limiting beliefs into the truth that sets me free? Would You reveal Jesus to me more clearly and intimately than I've ever known, drawing me close and never letting me go? Please show me how to walk with You, talk with You, and listen to You.

Thank you, loving Abba Father, Jesus, and Holy Spirit! Please help me see and be who You created me to be when You loved and formed me.

Chapter 1
Are You Eligible to be Joy-Full?

What Is Joy?

Joy is more than a human emotion! Jesus specified that the joy He speaks about is of divine origin, distinguishing spiritual fruit from happiness or worldly joy. The fruit of the Spirit listed as "joy" in traditional translations of the Bible is called "Exuberance about Life and God" in *The Message*, Galatians 5:22-23.

Spiritual joy doesn't depend on whether you're glad your children are wise or someone you love worships like you do. The fruit of joy isn't the result of being amused by a joke or a silly video, nor because your perfume smells great or you came up with clever or apt words.

Joy-filled exuberance that comes from God awakens you to the wonders of creation and the possibility of intimacy with the Creator, Savior, and Spirit of Truth. Although amusement and enjoyment may bring temporary pleasure, they pale compared to the reverent joy of embracing the beauty of life, your divine connection with God, and the anticipation of heavenly bliss.

The fruit of joy exceeds the fleeting pleasure of the "rocky ground" person who hears the word of God and at once receives it with pleasure, but it never takes root and only lasts a short time. It vanishes the moment trouble or opposition appears (Mark 4:5-6).

Instead, it's like the joy Jesus compares to the Kingdom of Heaven, like finding a treasure hidden in a field and, in joy and sacrifice, selling all you have to buy that field (see Matthew 13:45-46). It's the joy in recognizing the Son of God that had the as-yet-unborn John the Baptist leaping for joy in Elizabeth's womb (see Luke 1:44). It's the joy of the father of the prodigal son compassionately welcoming him back home, just as our Father in heaven longs to welcome the lost back home, at which all of heaven would join in rejoicing (Luke 15:7,20).

One of my Spiritual Direction School classmates and podcast guests, Gem Fadling, wrote: "Happiness isn't the ultimate goal—it's defined as feeling, showing or causing pleasure or satisfaction."[1] But it's often fleeting. Joy and contentment are wise, solid, unbending, and unwavering graces.

The Source of Joy

Our joy comes from the Father, the Son, and the Holy Spirit. When God's people enjoy a personal love relationship with Him and their hearts are truly committed to Him, God gives them joy, which then permeates not only the individual but also their homes (Acts 16:34).

The night before He died, Jesus told His disciples:

> "I am the vine; you are the branches. If you remain in me and I in you, you will bear much fruit; apart from me you can do nothing. ... If

---

[1] Gem Fadling, Why Happiness ISN'T the Ultimate Goal, www.unhurriedliving.com, published August 14, 2024, accessed October 2, 2024, *Continued in References.

you remain in me and my words remain in you, ask whatever you wish, and it will be done for you. ... As the Father has loved me, so have I loved you. Now remain in my love. If you keep my commands, you will remain in my love, just as I have kept my Father's commands and remain in his love. I HAVE TOLD YOU THIS SO THAT MY JOY MAY BE IN YOU AND THAT YOUR JOY MAY BE COMPLETE." ~ John 15:5,7,9-11 (emphasis added).

Of all nine aspects of the fruit of the Spirit, more Bible verses mention Joy than all the other fruits except Love and Peace. Joy is mentioned in 210 verses of the New International Version of the Bible!

My Joy-Full Holy Spirit Story

Christian coaches suggest telling your story about what God has done in your life with a simple formula: I used to be X; then Y happened; and now I'm Z. I can't do that. I've lived three-quarters of a century already. My Mom is 101, so I may just be entering my fourth quarter.

Much water has already flowed under my bridge, but I'm still paddling a canoe. Between the Before and the Now, there have been calm waters and rapids of conversion, growing, testing, backpaddling, and maturation. And I'm still God's work in process! So, I will share some meaningful stories and pray they touch your heart.

Before I became a true believer, long before I passed from middle age to "seasoned," I was, to all appearances, a successful attorney with a husband doing well in the real estate development arm of a local savings and loan. We were raising two adorable kids for whom I tried to be the perfect mother. I took time off to stay home until our youngest was four. When both were in school full days, I returned to practicing law, but with reduced hours.

My husband Toby and I were raised as Catholics. I stopped confessing my sins in college when I fell in love and gave into temptation, and I stopped attending Mass regularly at age twenty-one, falling into agnosticism. At thirty-five, I began to believe in God the Creator again after I experienced the miracle of childbirth. We had the kids baptized as infants, going through the expected motions.

A driven perfectionist, I was also a people-pleaser, prone to overwork, and a complainer about how tiring our life was. I felt overwhelmed, never "caught up," and rarely "free to relax." If I snuck out for a Saturday afternoon by myself—as scarce as a warm weather hailstorm—and came home to find the kids on the jungle gym and my husband reading on the patio, I'd angrily accuse him. I'd say, "You call that parenting? The kids are at least fifty feet away and could fall off that jungle gym and break their necks, but you wouldn't notice with your head buried in whatever you're reading!"

That described me on the morning of Saturday, September 8, 1989, although I was shorter on sleep than usual. A good friend had recently returned to Jesus and witnessed to me the preceding Thursday afternoon. She took me by the shoulders, shook me, and said, "It says in the Bible that if you're not *with* Jesus, you're against him. And you're not with Him, so if, like that swim team mom last week, you get hit by a truck and die, you're going to hell. So, please, as a favor to me, will you go to Confession and Mass on Saturday?"

I barely slept Thursday or Friday night, wondering if what she said was right. I got scared and decided that if I confessed, it would be like taking out a life insurance policy, and my friend would get off my back. I figured I'd at least get rid of accountability for my big sins. So, I spent much of that Saturday with a yellow legal pad (in my true lawyerly fashion) listing all the sins I could recall for the past two decades. (Toby asked to read my list; I said, "No way!") Then I left the house with him in charge for an hour.

To my utter surprise, when I confessed my sins, I was filled with remorse and sorrow for having offended God.

I cried holy tears. The priest gave me a shockingly light penance of one Our Father and said, "Welcome home."

I felt an enveloping peace wash over me from head to toe. I felt lighter than air. I practically floated out of the confessional, elated. I knelt and prayed briefly and then sauntered to my car. I thought, "A Mack truck can hit me now, and I'll be saved."

When I returned home, I walked around the side to the backyard and took in the sight. I opened my mouth to comment on the scene. Instead of the version I described above, I heard myself sweetly saying to Toby, "Isn't this a beautiful scene? The girls are playing so nicely with each other on the jungle gym, and after a hard week, you're getting to relax and enjoy reading *The New York Times*."

I was transformed!

The following morning, a Sunday, I told Toby that I'd start attending Mass on Sundays and would like to raise the kids in the faith, and I asked Toby how he felt. His father had taken him to Mass while his mother stayed home, and he didn't like the separation. So, he agreed to raise the kids Catholic with me, and off to church we went.

The next day, I bought a Bible and attended an Intercessory Prayer Group at a friend's home. She invited me to a charismatic prayer meeting that would be held later in the week. When I went to that meeting, where they spoke of the importance and the joy of baptism in the Holy Spirit, prayer group members offered to pray for anyone who hadn't yet received that joy. I asked for prayer, but those laying hands on me received the word that I had already been baptized in the Holy Spirit—in the confessional! Not long after, we had our civil marriage blessed in the Church.

Ever since, I have been on fire for God through the Holy Spirit, now thirty-five years and counting!

The Effects of Joy

Saint Paul prays in Romans 15:4 for hope, peace, and joy to strengthen and uplift us.

When our kids were in elementary school, my job at our parish's annual Vacation Bible School was leading the kids in praise and worship songs. The children's favorite song was based on Nehemiah 8:10, "Do not grieve, for the joy of the LORD is your strength." Based on that verse, the song begins with repeated lyrics about the joy of the Lord. Each verse consists of a single, catchy statement sung repeatedly. In the final verse, the kids mimicked laughter as they sang, and they'd invariably end up full of smiles or laughing out loud. Sweet and simple, the song encapsulates joy as a godly exuberance about life and God.

God is so pleased with our preference for a close relationship with Him that He wants to show His favor by shining light and joy on the upright in heart (Psalm 97:11). Similar to Acts 16:34 cited above, the Old Testament also shows the natural response to knowing that God is with you to help you: shouts of joy and victory will permeate the homes of followers who proclaim God's mighty and helpful works (Psalm 118:15 NASB).

Finding Joy

Alignment, abiding love, and surrender will bring you to joyful fulfillment of God's promises on earth and in the hereafter. Thanks be to God; you don't have to do that all by yourself!

You have access to the power of the Holy Spirit. You are supernaturally empowered ("clothed with power from on high") when you receive the Spirit of the living God and then walk by the Spirit (*cf.* Luke 24:49). And you have all this fruit in addition to joy: love, peace, patience, kindness, generosity, faithfulness, gentleness, and self-control (Galatians 5:22-23 NASB).

I enjoy comparing translations. *The Message*, Galatians 5, verses 22-23, describes the fruit of the spirit as "gifts ... like affection for others, exuberance about life, serenity ... willingness to stick with things, a sense of compassion in the heart, ... a conviction that a basic holiness permeates things and people ... loyal commitments, [and] not needing to force our way in life, able to marshal and direct our energies wisely."

When you live by this "spiritual fruit salad" (as Father Michael Hurley, O.P., Pastor of Saint Dominic Catholic Church in San Francisco, calls this list of spiritual attributes), you will not gratify the desires of the flesh (Galatians 5:16-17).

The desires of the flesh—the sinful nature or worldly cares—are just the opposite of what the Spirit wants, and vice versa. Worldly cares and desires "will keep you from inheriting the kingdom of God" (Galatians 5:16-17,21 NLT).

Therefore, while we still have the opportunity in this second half of life, let's live in response to the Spirit, "letting God's Spirit do the growth work" in us and harvest a crop of real, eternal life (Galatians 6:8 *The Message*). We'll harvest a good crop if we don't give up or quit (*id*.). This passage concludes with apt counsel, bearing in mind Saint Paul's advice that we should not try to do so much good that we get fatigued (*id.* at 9-10).

> "Right now, therefore, every time we get the chance, let us work for the benefit of all, starting with the people closest to us in the community of faith" (*id.*).

The interior matters most: expressing faith in love and not falling out of grace (Galatians 5:4-6, *The Message*).

It all boils down to yielding to God's plan: letting go of control, surrendering to God's will, and letting God show us the way to love.

Surrender and Humble, Simple Acts Are What Please God

Catholic Bishop Robert Barron beautifully shared God's way from the perspective of Saint Thérèse of the Child Jesus (who was called "The Little Flower" when my generation was growing up):

"What she offers is a "science of love," a way of knowing and acting that is utterly conditioned by the love that Jesus has placed in her heart: 'Jesus deigned to show me the road that leads to [heaven], and this road is the surrender of the little child who sleeps without fear in its Father's arms.'

[Thérèse concluded that **God] is pleased to work with those who have become utterly docile to his direction [and] acknowledged their total dependence upon him [and] their readiness to receive gifts. Any sense that God's love must be earned or that a relationship with him is a [transactional exchange] is repugnant to a healthy spirituality: 'Jesus does not demand great actions from us but simply surrender and gratitude.'**

When this attitude is in place, anything and everything is possible. Following Thérèse, **we can be pleasing to God and valuable to the Church in the humblest places and through**

the simplest acts. All we need to do is surrender, like a little child asleep in its Father's arms ..."[2]

What's the Impact of Beliefs and Spiritual Principles?

Why do we do what we do?

Do we put listening to and obeying God first? If not, why not?

Are we living by external standards: some "rules" we absorbed growing up or set for ourselves to go along with an image or drivenness not to make mistakes?

What about, "If it's worth doing, it's worth doing well" and the corollary, "If I can't do it well, I shouldn't do it at all?"

What about how we came to understand putting our self-care first as selfishness (though self-care is not

---

[2] Bishop Robert Barron, The Word on Fire Ministries, October 1, 2024, (emphasis added) *See References at the back of the book.

unlike a mother putting on her oxygen mask before putting one on a child in an airline emergency)?

There is great power in your mind and the spiritual principle of **BELIEF**. As a person thinks in her heart, so it is! (Proverbs 23:7 NKJV). Here are other examples of the principle of Belief at work.

In Matthew 9:29 (NLT), Jesus asked, "Do you believe I can make you see?"

"Yes, Lord," they told Him, "we do."

Then He touched their eyes and said, "Because of your faith, it will happen."

In Mark 9:23 (NLT), a father seeking deliverance and healing for his son asked Jesus if He could do anything for the boy. "If you can?" Jesus asked. "Anything is possible if a person believes."

In other words, we can expect to receive what we believe, say, and act on. Beliefs are like the human brain's software, and we tend only to notice what seems to agree with our beliefs. Therefore, embedded lies that we believe effectively become self-fulfilling prophecies.

According to the spiritual principle of **CORRESPONDENCE,** the way you measure out is how things will be measured out to you. We see this in teachings about receiving judgments about ourselves if we judge others (Luke 6:37). The Lord encourages us to follow the Golden Rule—treating others as we wish to be treated (Luke 6:31). The Lord's Prayer and following verses that point out if you refuse to forgive others, the Father will not forgive your sins (Matthew 6:14-15 NLT). In a few words, the principle of Correspondence means each of us will be judged, treated, or forgiven the same as we act in this life.

The spiritual principle of **HONESTY** calls us to keep our thoughts, words, and deeds fully aligned so that nothing we say contradicts what we think or do. In that case, we may walk fearlessly in the truth, which sets us free. This means you are living as the REAL you! The key verse supporting this principle is John 8:31-32: "If you hold to my teaching, you are really my disciples. Then you will know the truth, and the truth will set you free."

Similarly, "We will speak the truth in love, growing in every way more and more like Christ" (Ephesians 4:15 NLT). "Honesty guides good people; dishonesty destroys treacherous people" (Proverbs 11:3 NLT). And from the Parable of the Sower and the Seed: "The seeds that fell on the good soil represent honest, good-hearted people who hear God's word, cling to it, and patiently produce a huge harvest" (Luke 8:15 NLT).

The spiritual principle of **MANIFESTATION** tells us, in simple words, that what we focus on most and believe God for is most likely to manifest.

In the Old Testament, Psalm 37:4 says, "Take delight in the LORD, and he will give you the desires of your heart" (Psalm 37:4). In the Gospel, Jesus says, "Ask and it will be given to you; seek and you will find; knock and the door will be opened to you. For everyone who asks receives; the one who seeks finds; and to the one who knocks, the door will be opened (Matthew 7:7-8 (talking about those who believe and obey)).

James 1:6-7 NIV and 1:8 NLT say, "When you ask, you must believe and not doubt, because the one who doubts is like a wave of the sea, blown and tossed by the wind. That person should not expect to receive anything from the Lord. Their loyalty is divided between God and the world, and they are unstable in everything they do." More positively put, "Whatever is true, noble, right, pure, lovely, admirable—if anything is excellent or praiseworthy—think about such things. And the God of peace will be with you" (Philippians 4:8).

I suggest intentionally applying those principles to manifest more joy in your life:

1. Believe that with God's help, you can abide in God like a branch attached to the vine and bear the good fruit of the Spirit, including joy, and your joy can grow into complete joy.

2. Act in accordance with the Golden Rule: See Christ in everyone, respect them, show kindness and gentleness, forgive others, and then confidently ask God to forgive you.

3. Honesty requires identifying and eliminating any lies that influence you. Aligning your beliefs, thoughts, actions, and words with the Truth and values of God relates directly to abiding in God and ensuring that you are the REAL you.

4. Focus on delighting in the Lord, manifesting those desires you believe God put on your heart, seeking first God and His will for you and the Kingdom, and cultivating intimate (conversational) relationships with the Holy Trinity.

If you would like to learn eleven quickly grasped spiritual principles that helped me understand why certain things were happening in my life and how I could effect changes with unilateral action, visit *www.RadiantJoy.us/joy-book* and download my Spiritual Principles PDF as part of your gift package.

What Are the Three A's of Joy?

Complete Joy requires that we **ABIDE**—that is, remain in the Father's love while seeking and acting in accord with His will and His word in everything, knowing that He is Love and is always for you. The very elderly Joshua told this to Israel's elders, leaders, judges, and officials: "The Lord your God fights for you, just as he promised. So be very careful to love the LORD your God" (Joshua 23:2-5, 10-11).

31

ALIGNMENT with God, which happens in our Abiding, is so vital that Jesus taught His followers to pray, beginning with "Our Father in heaven, hallowed be your name, your kingdom come, your will be done, on earth as it is in heaven" (Matthew 6:9-10).

We must also align our inner selves—our beliefs, thoughts, and self-talk—with our outer behavior, actions, responses, and the Way, the Truth, and the Life of Jesus. Then we will be **AGLOW** with the Light of life and we will Radiate Joy.

Abide.

Align.

Aglow.

PRAYER

O God, Source of Joy, thank You that I can count on Your grace to draw me closer to You and to joy through faith, simple acts, surrender, and gratitude. Thank You for choosing me to be a member of Your Kingdom and to enjoy personal relationships with You, Sovereign Father, with King Jesus, and with the Holy Spirit. Would You please lead me and help me learn to manifest more joy through spiritual principles and love? Please guide me to abide with You and to align myself with the Way, the Truth, and the Life of Jesus, so I may be aglow with Your light, love, and joy. I need You and love You, Lord!

REFLECTION QUESTIONS
(For individual use or with a small group)

1. What comes to mind when you think about "joy" or "joy-filled" experiences in your life? How do you distinguish the joy of the Lord and happiness?

2. What's your response to hearing that God is so pleased when we want a close relationship with Him that He wants to show favor by shining light and joy on those of upright hearts? Are you prone to shouts of joy and victory and proclaiming what he's done for you, as the Old Testament describes?

3. How have you related to the Vine and Branches metaphor? Reflect on a time when you knew, felt, or experienced abiding in God and God in you, as a branch attached to the vine, such that your heart wanted to obey, follow, and love God. Did you ever know or feel (even temporarily) that His joy was complete in you for some time?

4. How do you respond to hearing that alignment, abiding love and surrender will

bring you to joyful fulfillment of God's promises, and that you don't have to do all that by yourself, because grace is available to you?

5. Were you already familiar with the spiritual principles of Belief, Correspondence, Honesty and Integrity, and Manifestation? Why are they important?

Chapter 2
Was Jesus Joyful?

Yes! Joy was Jesus' nature. He promised:

> *"If you keep my commands, you will remain in my love. ... I have told you this so that my joy may be in you and your joy may be complete. My command is this: Love each other as I have loved you." ~John 15:10-12*

Of course, Jesus took delight in creation. Why wouldn't he? If you've created a piece of art, music, writing, a fine meal, a craft, or a performance that satisfied your creative soul, you most likely experienced joy in the outcome, perhaps even acknowledging the role of the Spirit in its inspiration or execution.

We know from Scripture that Jesus took time to pray in secluded spots—for extended times of solitude with His Father, to escape the crowds, to receive direction, and for His own restoration and refilling, I suppose.

Perhaps it gave Him joy to observe the sun rising over a distant hill, revel in the mountains, overlook the valleys, admire the fields, smell the forests, listen to the sea, feel a warm breeze, or watch the sunlight sparkling over the Sea of Galilee.

Joy at Sinners' Repentance

If keeping His commands feels disheartening because you know you don't always do what Jesus commands, focus on God's mercy! During His days of public ministry, Jesus made it clear how much He and the Father experience joy when sinners repent and come to faith. In Luke 15, Jesus tells the Parable of the Lost Sheep, pointing out that tax collectors and other notorious sinners often came to listen to Him teach. Jesus told them:

> "If a man has a hundred sheep and one of them gets lost, what will he do? Won't he leave the ninety-nine others in the wilderness and go to search for the one that is lost until he finds it? And when he has found it, he will joyfully carry it home on his shoulders. When

he arrives, he will call together his friends and neighbors, saying, 'Rejoice with me because I have found my lost sheep.'"

He concluded:

"In the same way, there is more joy in heaven over one lost sinner who repents and returns to God than over ninety-nine others who are righteous and haven't strayed away!" ~Luke 15:3-10, NLT.

Joy in Healing with the Holy Spirit

Seeing effective healing prayer also gave Jesus joy. In Acts of the Apostles, chapter 10, verse 38, we hear that Father God anointed Jesus with the Holy Spirit and power, by which Jesus went around doing good works and healing all who were under the control of the devil.

Indeed, according to the Gospel of Matthew, Jesus' public ministry didn't start until the Spirit descended upon Him like a dove when He was baptized by John the Baptist and the Father spoke over Him: "This is my beloved Son, with whom I am well pleased" (Matthew 3:16 ESV).

From then on, Jesus performed countless healing miracles and drove out unclean spirits. Before His Passion, Jesus told His disciples that He was going away to His Father's house to prepare a place for them (John 14:2 ESV). In the conversation that followed, Thomas and Philip showed that they really hadn't comprehended Jesus' message, yet in the face of their confusion, Jesus declared:

> "Truly, truly, I say to you, whoever believes in me will also do the works that I do; and greater works than these will he do, because I am going to the Father. Whatever you ask in my name, this I will do, that the Father may be glorified in the Son. If you ask me anything in my name, I will do it. If you love me, you will keep my commandments. And I will ask the Father, and he will give you another Helper, to be with you forever, even the Spirit of truth, whom the world cannot receive, because it neither sees Him nor knows Him. You know him, for he dwells with you and will be in you."
> ~John 14:12-17 ESV.

In other words, Jesus promised the Holy Spirit. He foretold that obedient believers would ask for supernatural occurrences and have their prayers answered, and this would manifest the power of the Spirit of God.

Essentially, the message is: What *you* do isn't the key to joy, for *you* don't actually do what is supernaturally accomplished; you call upon the authority of Jesus' name. That heavenly power does the work, but it happens through you because of your faith and your loving, obedient relationship with Jesus. And it gives you great joy to be part of healing, generosity, and deliverance miracles. All glory to God. After twelve years of serving in healing and deliverance ministry, I certainly love that grateful, joyous feeling!

Joy in Followers Bringing Others to Him

When you and I influence other people to get closer to being converted, healed, forgiven, or set free, that brings joy to Jesus and us. For example, Jesus sent out seventy-two disciples to witness and pray with people in towns and villages. He knew that some of those towns would be unreceptive, and the disciples were to shake the dust from their feet and move on when they encountered strong resistance. But, to receptive people, they ministered (even before they'd been fully empowered on Pentecost). Look at the conversation they had with Jesus afterward, in Luke 10:17-20 (NLT):

> "When the seventy-two disciples returned, they joyfully reported to him, 'Lord, even the demons obey us when we use your name!'
>
> 'Yes,' he told them [referring to the war in heaven described in Revelation 12:7], 'I saw Satan fall from heaven like lightning! *Look, I have given you authority over all the power of the enemy, and you can walk among snakes and scorpions and crush them. Nothing will injure you.* But don't rejoice because evil spirits obey you; rejoice because your names are registered in heaven'" (emphasis added).

The disciples didn't experience that joy alone. Verse 21 tells us that, at the same time, Jesus was filled with the joy of the Holy Spirit, and He prayed in thanksgiving, "O Father, Lord of heaven and earth, thank you for hiding these things from those who think themselves wise and clever, and for revealing them to the childlike. Yes, Father, it pleased you to do it this way" (Luke 10:21, NLT).

Bringing Joy to Others Through His Presence

Jesus inspired joy in others' lives, and He is the model for us to follow! When Mary visited her pregnant older relative Elizabeth, the presence of Jesus in her womb caused John to leap for joy in his mother's womb (Luke 1:41). When Mary and Joseph presented Jesus in the temple, Jesus brought great joy to the elders Simeon and Anna, who had long awaited the Messiah and recognized the Messiah in the infant Jesus (Luke 2:25-38).

Jesus brought immense joy to the two he encountered on the road to Emmaus, because he listened to them as they walked along, opened the Scriptures to them, accepted their invitation to stay with them longer, and broke bread with them (Luke 24:13-35). And the two then spread that immense joy by walking the seven miles back to Jerusalem to tell the apostles what they'd experienced, and while they were there, Jesus appeared to His disciples (Luke 24:36).

Joy in Miracle-Working

Jesus brought joy not only to those He healed or cast demons out of but also to those who witnessed these miracles: the leper in Luke 5:13-16, the Canaanite woman whose demon-possessed daughter was set free in Matthew 15:21-28, and the father who asked Jesus to help his unbelief in Mark 9:20-26 when he brought Jesus his mute son who was convulsing and foaming at the mouth. Imagine the joy Jesus instilled in the Roman centurion when his servant was healed without Jesus going to his town or entering under his roof (Matthew 8:5-13).

Then there's the joy for the families and friends of those He resurrected from death, like Jairus and his young daughter in Luke 8:49-56 and Lazarus and his sisters Mary and Martha in John 11:38-44.

I experienced miraculous healing when friends laid hands on me and prayed for the healing of a pelvic condition diagnosed as requiring invasive surgical correction. The praying friends and I were overjoyed.

I have also prayed for other people for inner and physical healing, and the Lord has often brought the requested healing and some surprise healings those seeking prayer didn't even mention or ask to have healed. Receiving miraculous physical healing certainly builds up faith, trust, and joy! Indeed, Jesus didn't pray to the Father *asking for* physical healing; He *commanded* physical healing to occur, as did not only the apostles but other believers such as Ananias in Acts 9:17! Again, let's remember that Jesus left us this astonishing promise:

> "Very truly I tell you, whoever believes in me will do the works I have been doing and they will do even greater things than these, because I am going to the Father" (John 14:12).

Joy in Showing Love to Outcasts

Jesus also brought joy to sinners, such as the woman caught in adultery. Can you sense the feelings in the woman and the crowd of accusers when Jesus said to let someone without sin cast the first stone in John 8:7? And when her accusers left, Jesus did not condemn her.

How about when He knew the truth about the Samaritan woman at the well and, in John 4:18, told her about her husbands and about living water? She was so transformed that she told the whole town about the Messiah, even though she had formerly avoided the townspeople out of shame.

In Luke 19:5-9 (NLT), Jesus passed through Jericho, and a short tax collector named Zacchaeus climbed a sycamore tree to get a glimpse of Him. Jesus spoke to him, surprising him and probably everyone else, because people assumed tax collectors regularly skimmed part of the tax revenue for themselves. Jesus invited Himself to dinner that night at Zacchaeus' house. Zacchaeus hurriedly came down and took Jesus to his house in great excitement, receiving Him with joy (Luke 19:6 DRB).

Joy in His Passion, Ascension, and Resurrection

Joy in the Lord leads to praise so strong and deserved that Mother Nature will sing praise if God's people are silenced! On Palm Sunday, as Jesus made His way into Jerusalem on a colt, the crowd of disciples joyfully shouted praise to God for all the miracles they had seen. When some Pharisees told Jesus to rebuke His disciples, Jesus replied, "I tell you ... if they keep quiet, the stones will cry out" (Luke 19:35-40).

Many Christians may have skipped over the fact that despite all the anguish and physical agony of Jesus' passion, *with joy* Jesus endured the cross, despising the shame, taking all the past, present, and future sins of the world upon Himself (Hebrews 12:1-2 ESV). Hebrews 12, verses 2, 3, and 7 put it like this:

> "For the joy set before him, he endured the cross, scorning its shame, and sat down at the right hand of the throne of God. Consider him who endured such opposition from sinners, so that you will not grow weary and lose heart. ... Endure hardship as discipline; God is treating you as His children. For what children are not disciplined by their father?"

Of course, the joy in Jesus' resurrection and the appearances of the Risen Lord are unparalleled. In Luke 24:17, Jesus appears to Mary Magdalene, who is overjoyed and wants to hold onto Him. That evening, He appeared to ten of the apostles and the women who were with them. When He showed them His hands and feet, they initially did not believe what they saw. Why? "Because of joy and wonder," the Gospel of Luke reports in chapter 24:41-42 (NLT).

Then, at His Ascension, His disciples saw Him lift His hands and bless them, and then they saw Him being taken up into heaven. Their response was to worship Him and return to Jerusalem with great joy.

They stayed continually at the temple, praising God (Luke 24:51-53). And then they waited in obedience until the joy of Pentecost transformed them all!

Let's not overlook that joy is part of Jesus' nature, and He wants us to have complete joy! But, there are conditions.

Joy, Keeping Jesus' Commands, and The Way

Let's re-read this pivotal passage: "If you keep my commands, you will remain in my love ... I have told you this so that my joy may be in you and your joy may be complete. My command is this: Love each other as I have loved you" (John 15:10-12). Jesus said to lay down your life—that is, die to your selfish or worldly desires. He also said to do what He commands. (John 15:14).

Yes, the condition is to obey His commands, specifically the command to love one another. The primary benefit of keeping His commands is complete joy! And a part of that is receiving what you pray for as an obedient believer, probably someone in a two-way, intimate relationship with

God. God chose and appointed us to bear lasting fruit. In that context of bearing the fruit God created us for, Jesus said, "Whatever you ask in my name the Father will give you" (John 15:16-17).

I hear many people speak of what they do for God, and I've used that phrase as well, but when we consider what Jesus said about bearing good and lasting fruit, we don't do that *for* God but *with* God. And like Jesus, who had complete trust in the Father, we must also trust God wholeheartedly.

Jesus is the Way (John 14:6). While approximately 2.4 billion people identify themselves as Christians, sadly, most of the world does not,[3] and the percentages have been going against Jesus in the United States, declining from 91% of Americans identifying as Christians in 1976 to 64% of Americans in 2022.[4] If, as a well-known old hymn proclaimed, observers will know we are Christians by our love, the declining number of new believers

---

[3]Pam Wasserman, Population Education, "World Population by Religion: A Global Tapestry of Faith, PopEd Blog, January 12, 2024, https://populationeducation.org/world-population-by-religion-a-global-tapestry-of-faith/, accessed October 7, 2024.

[4] Decline of Christianity in the Western world. (2024, September 18). In *Wikipedia*. https://en.wikipedia.org/wiki/Decline_of_Christianity_in_the_Western_world, accessed October 7, 2024.

suggests that more Christians should love the way Jesus modeled. He warned us:

> "Do to others whatever you would like them to do to you. This is the essence of all that is taught in the law and the prophets. You can enter God's Kingdom only through the narrow gate. The highway to hell is broad and its gate is wide for the many who choose that way. But the gateway to life is very narrow and the road is difficult, and only a few ever find it." ~Matthew 7:12-14 (NLT)

In the Introduction, I spoke of Jesus as a radical, a model of the Way, who set a very high standard that we are meant to imitate.

Saint Paul told the Ephesians:

> "Be imitators of God in everything you do, for then you will represent your Father as his beloved sons and daughters. And continue to walk surrendered to the extravagant love of Christ, for he surrendered his life as a sacrifice for us. His great love for us was pleasing to God, like an aroma of adoration—

a sweet healing fragrance." ~Ephesians 5:1-2 TPT.

The Second Letter to Timothy also encourages us to let the faith and the love of Christ be our model (2 Timothy 1:13 NASB).

How Are We to Imitate Jesus?

Cultivate a Listening Relationship – Be Open to Hearing and Aligning With God's Will and Directions.

First, we need to be in a relationship conducive to listening to God so He can express love and guide us. We need to stay connected and remain open to hear the voice and discern the will of God. We also need to follow through in love and trust as we do what God says. Loving, spending time with God as Jesus did with the Father, being open to hearing Him, and taking His commands seriously are how we best imitate Christ.

Submit and Depend on God for Everything.

Many of us learned to value independent thinking. In our spiritual maturity, however, we learn to rely not on our understanding nor to be attached to our ways instead of God's ways. The wisdom of Proverbs 3:6 urges us, "In all your ways submit to him, and he will make your paths straight."

God supports, provides and enables those who carry out His mission in the Kingdom, like Abraham, Moses, David, the prophets, and the apostles. Like Jesus, we must also understand and accept our dependence on God for everything. Even He relied on God the Father. Jesus explained to the Jews trying to kill Him for breaking the Sabbath, "Very truly I tell you, the Son can do nothing by himself; he can do only what he sees his Father doing because whatever the Father does, the Son also does" (John 5:19).

We do not belong to ourselves, for Jesus bought us at a high price (1 Corinthians 6:19-20 NLT). We owe every breath to God (see Acts 17:25). We must not rely on ourselves but on God (2 Corinthians 1:9). You may have heard the saying, "God doesn't call the qualified; He qualifies the called." That maxim is based on 2 Corinthians 34-5 (NLT), where Saint Paul says confident witnessing came through Christ and the Spirit of the living God (2 Corinthians 3:4) for "It is not that we are qualified to do anything on our own. Our qualification ["competence" in the NIV] comes from God" (2 Corinthians 3:5 NLT).

Walk With (Lean or Depend On) Your Helper, the Holy Spirit.

Jesus is our model, but we need the Holy Spirit, too! We are not on our own to figure anything out because the indispensable Holy Spirit comes to guide us.

Also called the Spirit of Truth, He reveals the Truth and reminds us of truths we already know. The Spirit can clarify what's happening and tell us what is yet to come (John 16:13-14). He will come into our hearts and show us Jesus as the living Son of God, the anointed one, the Messiah, the Healer, the Redeemer, the One who will satisfy the deepest longing in our hearts. He is also the giver of gifts, and walking with Him yields excellent fruit (John 15:1-11).

Refrain from Defensive, Aggressive Behavior; Bear Suffering with Joy.

Peter describes this standard of imitating Jesus for Christians living among pagans. He teaches that disciples are to follow in Christ's footsteps because Christ suffered for us (1 Peter 2:21). Some basic behaviors which He didn't do and calls us not to do, are so foundational that we learned them as children: not sinning, lying, insulting, or threatening, even while suffering or being abused (*id.*).

What He calls us to do is to entrust ourselves to the Father, the righteous Judge. Believe Jesus carried our sins to the cross so we might die to sin and live for righteousness. Believe He healed us by His wounds so we might turn to Him to resist our symptoms or illnesses and be conduits of His healing to others. Also, accepting that He is the shepherd and guardian of people who continually stray, speak of and model Jesus to the lost. (1 Peter 2:21-25, NASB).

Being Christlike is what we're meant to do as God's love for us and ours for Him move us. That doesn't mean that we have to be sinless and without weakness to "earn salvation."

We are to act and to believe based on who we are in Christ, who we believe Him to be, and out of our desire to abide in Him through listening and responding as He asks.

Accordingly, faith and works go together (*see* James 2:18 ESV). As Saint Paul says, "The only thing that counts is faith expressing itself through love" (Galatians 5:6).

You may have been taught to "offer it up" and welcome the message of God during severe suffering. When you offer your suffering for the redemption of others or the salvation of the world, not only is that a powerful prayer, but you'll also be walking with the Holy Spirit, and you'll receive the fruit of joy in honor of your sacrifice.

In 1 Thessalonians 1:6-7 (NLT), Saint Paul says:

"You became imitators of us and of the Lord, for you welcomed the message in the midst of severe suffering, with the joy given by the Holy Spirit. And so you became a model to all the believers."

We all fall short of God's high standard (Romans 3:23). Praise be to God, who is compassionate and merciful (Psalm 145:8)! We can repent, and we are forgiven (Acts 5:31). Our sins are then gone far from us and God (Psalm 103:12).

God wants us to be co-heirs with Jesus, adopted children, and to draw near the throne of grace with confidence, to receive mercy and grace (Romans 8:17; Hebrews 4:14-16 ESV). Christ's victory is ours (*see* 1 John 5:4).

Don't let talk of obedience dishearten you because you know you don't always do what Jesus commands; focus on God's mercy! By the blood of Jesus you are holy, so believe that and make choices compatible with holiness.[5]

---

[5] Matt Lozano, *Free to Be Holy*, 2023, The Word Among Us Press, Frederick, MD, page 27 (Jesus' sacrifice makes us holy and we can't try to be holy apart from Him).

Recognize Your Human Weaknesses and How God Strengthens You.

Oddly, it's great to know that we are weak and flawed because that's when we're most likely to call on the Lord for help and His supernatural strength. And when God then provides the strength and what we couldn't do on our own comes to fruition, we are joyful!

Philippians 3 warns us not to put our confidence in the flesh, our human nature. Instead, Saint Paul tells his followers:

> "Rejoice in the Lord!" ... We who serve God by his Spirit ... who put no confidence in the flesh ... consider everything a loss because of the surpassing worth of knowing Christ Jesus ... I do not consider myself yet to have taken hold of it. But one thing I do: Forgetting what is behind and straining toward what is ahead, I press on toward the goal to win the prize for which God has called me heavenward in Christ Jesus. All of us, then, who are mature should take such a view of things ... Those whose god is their stomach ... their mind is set

on earthly things. But our citizenship is in heaven." ~Philippians 3:1,3,8,13-15.

More succinctly, Saint Paul told the Romans and the Galatians:

"For I know that good itself does not dwell in me, that is, in my sinful nature. For I have the desire to do what is good, but I cannot carry it out" (Romans 7:18).

"For the flesh desires what is contrary to the Spirit, and the Spirit what is contrary to the flesh. They are in conflict with each other, so that you are not to do whatever you want" (Galatians 5:17).

The actionable point is this: "Delight in weaknesses, in insults, in hardships, in persecutions, in difficulties. For when [you are] weak, then [you are] strong" (2 Corinthians 12:1). Indeed, the promise is that you can do all things through Christ who strengthens you (Philippians 4:13 ESV).

Recognizing our human weakness even helps with that tough challenge for many women: managing our time and our energy. We may tend to focus on lack. But the joy of the Lord is our strength (Nehemiah 8:10). The prophet Habakkuk painted a dire world picture of lack, crop and flock failures, and barrenness, and in the same breath, he declared:

> "Yet I will rejoice in the LORD!
> I will be joyful in the God of my salvation!
> The Sovereign LORD is my strength!
> He makes me as surefooted as a deer,
> able to tread upon the heights.
> ~Habakkuk 3:17-19.

Surrendering and Letting God Have His Way

From the Old Testament, we also learned that we are clay in the hands of the potter (Isaiah 64:8.) Apostle Paul clarifies that though we are merely clay, there are treasures in the clay jars (2 Corinthians 4:7). I've seen clay that my grandchildren have— especially Play-Doh®. It's nothing but "potential" while it's in the container, but it is molded into "treasures" of their imaginative creativity when they work it with their hands or even use a cookie cutter to break it apart and make it conform to their intentions.

God also shapes and molds us to show that supernatural power belongs to God and not to us (*id.*). Knowing that this is what God will do with us, along with the wisdom of Proverbs 3:5, encourages us to rely not on our own understanding but on Him. We are to acknowledge God and let God have His way with us.

In this way, we don't boast about or proclaim ourselves; instead, we declare that Jesus is Lord, and we are His instruments, hopefully, available for His purposes. One important purpose is to let the light which God has shone in our hearts shine out of darkness (*id.* at 5-6). When combined with joy, that light becomes Radiant Joy that attracts and blesses others and yourself.

Kingdom People Must Remain Loyal to the Sovereign

Early in the gospels and Christ's public ministry, we hear bold proclamations that the Kingdom of God is in our midst and even within us. As God's chosen people, we are members of the royal family of God (1 Peter 2:9) with full access to His love, favor, and joy. Being daughters of God, the Sovereign King of all creation, we are princesses of the Most High.

We have exceptional rights and privileges (the ability to enter the King's presence), dignity (because of the King's favor), and of course, royal responsibilities (such as showing active love to the little ones, the least of the brethren). In return for being in this royal family of God, we are expected to live according to King Jesus' Way, Truth, and Life, frequently gathering with others in the royal family of the King who reigns over all the nations.[6]

Like Britain's Prince Harry and Meghan Markle, the Duke and Duchess of Sussex, God's children and their family members get to choose whether they want to be Kingdom people! To be loyal to the kingdom, children of the King must give up certain worldly pursuits and yield their wills to the sovereign.

Prince Harry and Meghan weren't looking to step down as senior members of the royal family after their son was born, but they wanted different roles

---

[6] See Luke 17:21, 18:16-17 (NIV and DRB); Psalm 82:6; 1 Thessalonians 3:9; Acts 7:46; Luke 18:16; John 14:6; Acts 14:27; Psalm 47:8.

because of intense press coverage and security concerns. They had hoped to split their time between Canada and the UK and launch some commercial ventures for financial independence.[7]

But loyal royals cannot refuse to suffer. Indeed, to enter the kingdom and rise with the king, a person must also accept possible adverse attacks, perhaps even persecution. But the destiny of Kingdom people includes dining at the King's banquet table, seeing Him face-to-face, and even sitting with Him on the throne (*cf.* Luke 22:29-30).

Everyone is called to enter God's Kingdom, but there are what economists might call "barriers to entry." The Creator made us intelligent creatures with free will. He allows us to enter into the divine plan by our actions, prayers, and sufferings, becoming co-workers for His Kingdom.[8] It's important to know, however, that even as the King's creatures, we cannot attain our ultimate end without the help of His grace.[9]

---

[7] See Reference page at the back of the book for details.
[8] 1 Corinthians 3:9, 1 Thessalonians 3:2; Colossians 1:24, 4:11.
[9] Matthew 19:25-26; John 15:6; 14:13.

Adopt a Godly Mindset by Trusting God for Everything

We can view a "Godly Mindset" from two angles.

First, there's the inner work of resetting your mind to approximate Christ's Mind. This sounds impossible, but it has to be possible, or the Bible would not contain these verses:

- "In your relationships with one another, have the same mindset as Christ Jesus: Who, being in very nature God, did not consider equality with God something to be used to his own advantage; rather, he made himself nothing by taking the very nature of a servant, being made in human likeness." (Philippians 2:5-7).

- "Thanks be to God through Jesus Christ our Lord! So then, I myself serve the law of God with my mind, but with my flesh I serve the law of sin" (Romans 7:25 ESV).

- "We have the mind of Christ" (1 Corinthians 2:16 NIV).

- "The god of this age [Satan] has blinded the minds of unbelievers, so that they cannot see the light of the gospel that displays the glory of Christ, who is the image of God" (2 Corinthians 4:4 NIV).

Let's remember those verses and trust that we can take our thoughts captive, trust God, and live from a godly perspective.

Second, if you're a believer who has surrendered everything to the Lord, you would seem to have God nearly always on your mind, considered in your decision-making, responding to circumstances and whatever is happening around you by sensing what Jesus living in you would do.

When you are so close to God, allowing God to take the reins and guide you so much that you're aware of Jesus and the Spirit living in you, the ensuing feeling must include not only joy but the other fruit: love, peace, patience, kindness, generosity, faithfulness, gentleness, and self-control (Galatians 5:22-23). With all those qualities, how could you be anything but delighted, glad, grateful, and *joyful*?

You will also have close relationships with each person of the Holy Trinity, even distinguishing their voices or promptings as they guide and direct your life—a connection by which you "Take delight in the LORD, and he will give you the desires of your heart" (Psalm 37:4).

PRAYER

Jesus, thank You for showing me that You experienced joy at sinners' repentance, finding the lost sheep, healing and miracle-working, showing love to outcasts, and even enduring Your passion and the Cross. Please help me embrace Your amazing promises, including the promise of the Holy Spirit and greater works! Have mercy on me. When I am weak, please be my strength. Grant, Lord, that I may imitate You yet understand that what I do isn't the key to joy, for it's only in Your name and authority and by the Holy Spirit's power that great fruit comes forth. May I be Your hands and mouth and feet as You call me? May I bear all my trials with joy, with Your strength? Help me, Jesus, to be more like You each day.

REFLECTION QUESTIONS
(For Individual Use or with a Small Group)

1. Consider Jeremiah 29:11 (NLT): "For I know the plans I have for you," says the LORD. "They are plans for good and not for disaster, to give you a future and a hope." Do you, like Jesus, trust in the Father who is for you and has a perfect plan that will bring you peace, security, and joy?

2. Acts 1:1 clarifies that all of Jesus' acts and teachings are the model for ours. He doesn't inspire only external and material imitation of His acts. How can we be like Jesus in what we believe and think, maintaining an interior temperament like His? What aspects of your mind will need to be transformed?

3. 2 Corinthians 13:9 says that whenever we are weak, God is strong. Reflect on a time when you had to rely on God's strength, and His strength came through for you.

4. Do you have an old habit of leaning on your own understanding or on other people for advice? Are you ready and willing to rely on

God instead? What will it take to start replying on God (rather than your own understanding) intentionally and regularly?

Chapter 3
How Can a Seasoned Woman Find Joy and Connection?

Jesus recognized the need for people to connect with one another.

He sent seventy-two disciples *two-by-two* to every place He was about to go (Luke 10:1). The Gospel shows neighbors and friends supporting others during times of celebration (the wedding at Cana) and grieving. A loud group had gathered at the home of the synagogue leader, Jairus, as his young daughter lay dying and then died. Although Jesus wanted to pray for the little girl out of the crowd's sight, He still had three of His disciples, the girl's parents, and Himself (six adults) gather together as He performed the miracle of raising the girl from death (Mark 5:38-42).

John tells us that "many Jews had come to Martha and Mary to comfort them in the loss of their brother (John 11:19)." On the cross, Jesus presented His mother to John, and John took her into his home so she would not be alone (John 19:27).

After the Resurrection, Jesus sent instructions for His disciples to wait for Him together, and there were over a hundred gathered in the Upper Room, including His mother and other women (Acts 1:4, 14-15).

First Corinthians, Chapter 12, describes different kinds of spiritual gifts and forms of service given to benefit one another within the Body of Christ (verses 4, 5, 7, and 12). And that body of believers is to have concerns for one another and share their joy (verses 25 and 26).

The early church was communal, usually meeting outdoors and in private homes (Acts 2:46). I've been blessed to experience communal faith sharing in my spiritual journey, and these connections have inspired my passion for the value of connecting with brothers and especially sisters in Christ.

Wisdom from Seasoned Women Navigating the Second Half Together

Because we are not meant to journey through life alone, and other seasoned women of faith are a treasure, I host groups through which we meet and connect deeply. We mainly connect on Zoom because of diverse locations, convenience, and because it works! In my free online conversations about Navigating the Second Half of Life, the ladies usually begin by sharing the surprises they've encountered in the transition or in this stage of their lives, often describing challenges that others in the group identify with.

The most commonly voiced challenges relate to health and physical well-being, where they live, changes in marital status, financial issues, attitudes and moods, or relationship and social situations they didn't anticipate.

Unsurprisingly, many speak of reduced energy, being unable to be on their feet as long as before, or getting quickly drained by active grandchildren. Sometimes, we become aware of our mortality like never before. Many of us have to be more intentional about exercise or physical therapy and recognize our need for complex dietary changes, perhaps for surgery. Maybe there's some brain fog or more frequent memory lapses. Vision may make driving at night unsafe. Balance could be an issue. Some are lonely, maybe living alone for the first time. Some are in a blended family or a multi-generational sandwich, with tugs to serve disparate family members, sometimes coast to coast.

Sometimes, older women want to avoid admitting that something they used to do easily is now tricky, particularly tech stuff and grunt work or beloved pastimes like needlework. Disappointment may arise when we do things the old way, which doesn't work as it used to.

On the other hand, people may assume we're sitting around at home in a rocking chair and can be available at any time. When we decline a request, we may hear, "Why not? You don't work." Often said to authors, artists, entrepreneurs, or women who have businesses, actively volunteer, or serve in a ministry, those remarks may trigger defensiveness. Many seasoned women put off a lot of interests in the first half and always hoped to pursue them in their second half!

Most of the women in my Wisdom Circles are serving God in some way, and they find it challenging when what they are doing as led by God is not accepted by those around them, maybe even by their husbands or offspring. Though they may also gather with friends with a shared interest, such as (for me) quilt-making or writing, they mostly enjoy or seek friendships with other believers.

Of course, it's sad to see loved ones not living with God-first principles, enmeshed in a world that appears to be far less honoring of Christianity than it was when we were younger. Most seasoned women would like to pass on wisdom to the younger generation, but we often find our adult kids unavailable to absorb what we want to share.

Yet, despite second-half surprises and challenges, these women usually say they wouldn't want to return to their younger years!

Faith-filled women appreciate the freedom to be themselves and to put God first, recognizing that that's not what many others are interested in. In their hearts—at least most of the time—they enjoy the love of God, the peace and trust, and the hope or confidence of eternal life. They know God, the most loving and powerful force in existence, is on their side, protecting, blessing, and providing for them.

Especially if you're retired from work and childrearing, it helps to think, "ALL my time is FREE, for it is for Freedom that Jesus set me free" (Galatians 5:1). When I realized that, I gave thanks for all the times I've felt torn, "behind," exhausted, and overwhelmed, for those feelings became learning tools to reveal what freedom is about. I don't work for God as a servant; rather, I have the calling, favor, and privilege of working with God, and I have free will and choice as to when and how much to do at any time. I choose to align with God's will, who lovingly works everything out for me per Romans 8:28!

A Time We're Unprepared For

The first quarter of life typically prepares us for the second quarter, focusing on socialization, family life, language and learning skills, education, identifying interests and possible careers, and, for many, embracing expectations for marriage and childrearing. Those expectations may or may not pan out, though what we envision influences what we get. (Remember the spiritual principle of Belief?) I hope you enjoyed a career and perhaps a family, built many more excellent relationships than the few that might have been bumpy (or worse), had a good roof over your head, and nutritious food to eat, physically and spiritually.

I have noticed that helpful, intentional preparation for the second half of life is often nonexistent or haphazard. Investment advisors, estate planners, therapists, pastors, and doctors may have offered good counsel, but we may have been too busy, set in our ways, or nonchalant to heed it.

One day, we might realize that the bigger house we splurged to buy for our growing family is now too big for us, has too many stairs, or is far away from our grandkids. So, we relocate or consider moving, but how will that affect our community of faith and social connections? We may find ourselves alone or lonely because of divorce, illness, or a sudden loss. Sometimes a life ends with no warning or preparation.

Many seasoned women are or have been caretakers for a loved one, and some have been widowed. Grieving is different for everyone, and our culture isn't very adept at comforting those who mourn, though that is one of the beatitudes.

For me and many, the death or disability of a husband or other loved one is our worst nightmare (especially when a medical emergency affects anyone dear to us, and even when we trust God).

For others, that's their actual life. My sister lost her husband in her forties when he had a fatal heart attack on the eve of his 50th birthday.

My husband was taken by ambulance to a hospital two hours away and had to have two heart stent procedures in his mid-sixties. Thank God, he was blessed to survive and thrive. I have also noticed that I've begun to need my husband's help more than I did when I was younger.

Sometimes even pondering our mate's death and disability leads us to wonder where we will live and how we will handle our daily lives in light of such changes. Even without worry or fear, and trusting the Lord has good plans, these thoughts can be part of the seasoned woman's thinking now in ways far more prevalent than in the first half of life.

Perhaps we expected to retire around sixty-five, but that was before an economic downturn wiped out much of our nest egg, or we ended up in jobs with no retirement benefits. So, we must decide on a frugal retirement or an extended work life, and we put off dreams of how much fun we'd be having on our retirement travels or adventures.

Of course, some women our age are re-energized. People define retirement differently, mostly as "not working." CNBC's August 2024 "Your Money" retirement survey found that among today's current generation of retired people, 71% report they're not working in any capacity. Of those who are working, more people elect to work, rather than work because they must. Of the segment currently saving for retirement, only 11% say they don't plan to work in any capacity after they retire, while more than half anticipate continuing to work either because they will want to or to supplement their income.[10]

Researchers at Morningstar ran retirement outcome models recently and concluded that 45% of U.S. households are likely to run out of money in retirement, but delaying full retirement shifts the odds in your favor. Just over a quarter of households, they say, will fall short in retirement if retiring at age seventy, compared to nearly half if retiring at sixty-five.[11]

A life full of energy, mental clarity, physical wellness, spiritual serenity and fulfillment may have felt out of reach lately, even if you still believe such a life IS possible. You may wonder about mental issues even more than physical functions. You can't remember names like you used to, nor retrieve a word or conversation on the tip of your tongue just a minute ago. And where the heck are your keys?

Health and well-being are uncertainties to surrender to God, while also taking wise

[10] Ryan Ermey, "Only 11% of American workers don't plan to work at all after they retire," September 6, 2024, MakeIt, LinkedIn, accessed September 6, 2024.
[11] *Id. citing* Spencer Look, associate director of retirement studies at Morningstar Retirement.

preventative or remedial action. My baby boomer friends have tended to remain active, unless or until they or their spouse needs a hip or knee replacement, a rotator cuff repair, back surgery, or something else that doesn't kill you but slows you down.

You may face far more subtle shifts. You don't like venturing into a room full of people of various ages and being ignored. You feel rather invisible—or worse, labeled as elderly. Toby and I attended a writers' workshop recently. When one participant shared her spontaneous writing, she described us as "an old married couple." I was so shocked, I blogged about it! Many of us wish we could wake up feeling refreshed each morning, having enjoyed a good night's sleep. Others wish they weren't as tired as they are, so they didn't need the naps they often take. Maybe you can't open jars, and your computer has become a bit of a technical nightmare with all the new bells and whistles.

In my group and individual conversations with women navigating the second half, it appears that many women tend to enter the second half primarily prepared through lessons gleaned from the school of hard knocks or untested assumptions. Comparisons can trip us up and are ungodly.

Thankfully, nothing is wasted with God! And the challenges are only one side of the coin. There are lots of blessings in this season of life as well. Sharing this aspect of our lives with others who relate and understand has proven to be cathartic, which is why I plan to continue offering online ways for seasoned Christian women to connect.

What Did You Expect and What Surprised You?

By their mid-fifties or beyond, women have been through many seasons, but that doesn't mean that we are now in the autumn of our lives, bearing our last fruit and getting ready for winter-like dormancy from here forward. No!

We still have seasons that the Lord may bring us to and guide us through. During health concerns or grieving a loss, God may want us to rest and be restored. Perhaps He then gets us ready for Him to restore the months or years the locusts have eaten and to begin again (*see* Joel 2:25). Perhaps He is equipping us to serve with a new reservoir of compassion and understanding, or even new skills and knowledge, or blessing us with new companions on the journey.

Others who are our age may never have slowed down yet! That's where I was pre-COVID. For me, the pandemic offered a consolidation of experiences, lessons learned, and maturity and wisdom gained. It was a season of prolific content creation, transformation, transition, and service that may potentially impact my family and (who knows?) the world.

For you, there may be a season in which you immerse yourself in your avocation, doing something you always wanted to do but couldn't fit in earlier. Opportunities like these might arise in a volunteer capacity helping people you always wanted to serve, a new entrepreneurial undertaking, or a different area of interest.

New opportunities arose in my life through writing and ministry. Part of that was because my seventy-one-year-old husband cares so much about his work serving a remote hospital that he cannot conceive of retiring; he continues to be begged to stay involved for years to come. We're grateful that most of his work is done from home.

God Didn't Only Have Plans For Us From Our Twenties Through Our Fifties!

Look at what He's said in Sacred Scripture and through Biblical examples of elders in the Bible.

Gray hair is a crown of glory or splendor; it is attained in the way of righteousness—also called "living a godly life" or "virtuous living" (Proverbs 16:31 NIV, NLT, NASB).

God may choose to use all the experiences we've lived through so far to give us hearts, minds, spirits, and bodies to best serve the calling He planned for us. In my service in healing and deliverance, spiritual direction, and transformational coaching, I regularly notice that God selects me to be the instrument He appoints to serve a person going through a hardship I've already endured, persevered through, learned and been healed from. It truly helps that "I get it" when they share their woes or challenges. The Holy Spirit leads me to ask questions that elicit the reflection, memory, or insight the person in front of me needs to acknowledge for their healing. God is so good.

I've spent years in a variety of coaching or leadership roles, which may, on the outside, seem like floundering from one interest to another. However, I look back on the years of doing that and see how it all culminated in who I am today and what skill set, experience, tools, and interests I now have in my arsenal. I've said it before: nothing is wasted with God, who knows exactly how to work all things together for good (John 6:12, Romans 8:28).

Blessings in the Second Half of Life

Second-half blessings may include grandparenting, more leisure time, increased time and intimacy with a spouse or for creativity, pastimes, travel, or service, and the luxury of more extended time for prayer and meditation. In this second half, you may intentionally implement boundaries or express your true self like never before. You can enjoy respect for your wisdom and experience. The freedom from a former job or career may open opportunities for ministry or entrepreneurial undertakings.

Hopefully, we've learned to die to ourselves, to ask and follow directions and guidance from God, and to trust in aligning ourselves to God's will and delight. If not yet, how about now? If we haven't done so already, it's time we surrender, leaving the results to God.

Seasoned women of faith tell me they appreciate the clarity and wisdom they have now more than ever! Many feel happier, more content, and more productive now than they used to. They understand their callings from God (why they're here on earth), and see how God equipped or qualified them and then multiplied their efforts supernaturally.

Many have done the spiritual inner work to learn to stop judging, comparing, and criticizing, and many now have the freedom to speak the truth in love without the compulsive people-pleasing that was their M.O. in prior decades. They finally understand the importance of forgiveness and the healing that comes from letting go. Some have come to know and relate to their adult kids better in this season of life. They recognize their unique giftedness and gladly share their gifts, insights, compassion, or hope with others, including strangers.

Many older women know that they've learned from their suffering of trials and adverse circumstances, and the Lord has used that to make them wiser, kinder, more compassionate—indeed, more like Christ than they were in their first half of life.

They recognize the power of having a relationship with the Father, Son, and Holy Spirit and listening to the Lord. They know the importance of embracing the truth that sets them free and accepting that spiritual principles determine outcomes. Many women in their second half of life feel blessed and want to share their faith with others, even if "only" through prayer.

They make it a point to surrender and to put on the mind of Christ, which uplifts those who do the work to heal, grow, and believe in God's promises, including the overarching Romans 8:28 (NASB) promise that God works all things for good for those who love God and are called according to His purposes.

From the Surrender Novena Given By Jesus to Father Dolindo Ruotolo

Saint Padre Pio of Pietrelcina (1887-1968) was an Italian priest and mystic known for his adoration of charity and love for the people around him. He bore the wounds of Christ for fifty years until they disappeared miraculously a few days before his death. Initially, he felt great humiliation at the painful, bleeding wounds, but he welcomed the pain for all of humanity. He was canonized in 2002 by Pope Saint John Paul II.[12]

For at least part of his life, Saint Padre Pio's spiritual director was a fellow Franciscan, Servant of God Father Dolindo Ruotolo (1882-1970) who offered himself as a victim soul for humanity and was blessed with prophecies, miracles, and conversations with Jesus.[13] Saint Padre Pio is known to have prayed the well-known nine-day Surrender Novena attributed to Don Dolindo.

The Surrender Novena begins with words from "Jesus to the soul" for each of the nine days, and each day ends with "Say 10 times: O Jesus, I surrender myself to You, take care of everything!" I dare to highlight the words that speak most convincingly to my heart:

---

[12] Biography, Padre Pio Foundation of America, https://padrepio.com/padre-pio/biography/, accessed October 17, 2024

[13] The Surrender Novena | Padre Pio Ministry to the Suffering, https://padrepioministry.org/surrender-novena/, accessed October 17, 2024

1. "Every act of true, blind, complete surrender to me produces the effect that you desire and resolves all difficult situations."

2. Don't fret, be upset, lose hope, or offer worried prayers. Worrying, being nervous, and thinking about consequences is against this surrender, like children whose childlike efforts get in their mother's way of seeing to their needs. Put yourself in Jesus' care so only He acts.

3. Don't pray for Jesus to act as you want, adapting your ideas. "Thy will be done on Earth as it is in Heaven" is seeking Jesus' intervention with all His omnipotence to resolve the most difficult situations.

4. Don't worry if you see evil growing, for if you don't worry, aren't upset, and surrender everything to Jesus, He will accomplish needed miracles.

5. Jesus will prepare you when He must lead you on a different path, carrying you like a sleeping child in her mother's arms. Your thoughts, worry, and desire to handle matters

yourself are what trouble and hurt you immensely.

6. Sleeplessness is related to wanting to judge, direct, and use your own human abilities or other humans' strength rather than trusting and resting in Jesus. Don't give in to Satan's agitation that removes you from Jesus' protection by throwing you into the "jaws of human initiative."

7. Jesus performs miracles in proportion to your full surrender. Trust in Him and don't think of yourself for all your needs, especially the most dire, and you'll see great, continual, silent miracles.

8. Let yourself be carried on the flowing current of grace, not thinking of the present or the future, but just believing in the Lord's love and promise that if you say, "You take care of it," He will, and He'll console, liberate, and guide you.

9. Even if you suffer, always pray and be ready to surrender, and you'll receive great peace and rewards. Humble yourself and fear not,

assured that "A thousand prayers cannot equal one single act of surrender."[14]

Elder Role Models

Have you been amazed at the ages of Old Testament characters? Starting with Genesis, one line suffices to illustrate the point: "Abraham fell facedown. Then he laughed and said to himself, 'Can a child be born to a man who is a hundred years old? Can Sarah give birth at the age of ninety?'" ~Genesis 17:17.

Moses was eighty years old, and Aaron was eighty-three, when they spoke to Pharaoh (Exodus 7:7), and by the time the Israelites got to the Red Sea after forty years of wandering, Moses had to be about 120! His successor was Joshua, and the LORD said to him, 'You are old and advanced in years, and there remains yet very much land to possess'" (Joshua 13:1). Saul was thirty when he became King of Israel and he reigned for forty-two years, making him seventy-two (2 Chronicles 26:1).

At the beginning of Jesus' life, when Mary and Joseph took Him to be presented to the Lord in the temple,

---

14 *Id.*

they were greeted by two elderly figures, Simeon and Anna. We don't know Simeon's age, but he was a devout man "waiting for the consolation of Israel," and the Holy Spirit had revealed to him that he wouldn't die before seeing the Messiah (Luke 2:25-26). After meeting Mary, Joseph, and Jesus, and prophesying to them, he said to God, "As you have promised, you may now dismiss your servant in peace. For my eyes have seen your salvation," which suggests he was not a healthy younger man (Luke 29-30). The prophet Anna was described as "very old," "a widow until she was eighty-four" (Luke 2:36).

The First Letter to Timothy contains a directive about how to treat "respectable" widows over sixty and elders "who do their work well" (1 Timothy 5:9-10, 17-19).

Assuming the apostle John was born early in the first century, he would have been over eighty when he wrote Second and Third John and between eighty and ninety years old when he wrote Revelation.[15]

One of my favorite saints is Saint Hildegard of Bingen because of her extensive visions, creativity, outspokenness (based on biographical books I've

---

[15] See References at the back of the book.

read about her), and her brilliance. She was a Benedictine abbess who founded monasteries and wrote theological, botanical, and medical works. She practiced medicine (primarily herbal medicine). She composed hymns, antiphons, liturgical drama, the oldest known morality play, and more! She was born around 1098 and lived (actively) until 1179, at around eighty-one years old. In 2012, she was designated a Doctor of the Church, in recognition of "her holiness of life and the originality of her teaching."[16]

Saint Teresa of Calcutta ("Mother Teresa") was active in her well-known Missionaries of Charity ministry until 1997, the year she died at eighty-seven.[17]

There is no reason any of us should be put out to pasture! Even if we have physical limitations, difficulties with transportation, or an age-related slowdown, we can still focus on having an optimal state of intimacy with God, being free in Christ, and

---

[16] See Wikipedia, Hildegard of Bingen,
https://en.wikipedia.org/wiki/Hildegard_of_Bingen, accessed October 6, 2024.
[17] Catholic Online, Saints & Angels, Saint Teresa of Calcutta, https://www.catholic.org/saints/saint.php?saint_id=5611, accessed October 6, 2024.

maintaining a positive self-image. We can seek meaningful strategies for connecting deeply with God—perhaps through Holy Communion or Eucharist, the communion of two-way dialogues, forgiveness and healing, belief work about God Himself and yourself, and possibly sharing or seeking guidance on embracing aging with grace and faith. Maybe creativity is calling to you! I'd like to encourage everyone: won't you step into your calling, embrace your identity in Christ, and live out your faith with boldness and confidence?

Within this second half, there are also shorter seasons. (I use the term "seasoned women" because we've been through many seasons, but also because alternative words such as older, senior, or "Baby Boomers" seemed to exclude or put off some people, even myself.) What season are you in right now?

Once when I asked God what season I was in, I heard in my spirit, a season of restoration, a time to honor my sacred self-care, have FUN with my writing, and start spreading the message about Radiant Joy—a stark contrast from when I asked what season I was in before. That time, I sensed the message, "Striving is what you were doing, and you were not at peace."

I followed up with questions about what I'd need to cut back on or eliminate to have enough time for what's new this season, and I received six specifics, along with some other changes in my environment and scheduling to give writing the priority it needed. Another time, He called my season a time of preparation, planting seeds to be watered for harvesting later. What season you're in is a useful question to bring to the Lord periodically.

Do you believe that a woman in her second half of life can be vibrantly joyful?

What if she were to embrace her true identity, adopt a Jesus mindset, and live in unity with the Trinity? Many of us learned that God created us to know, love, and serve Him in this world and to be happy with Him forever in the next.[18] Embracing that rubric remains a simple way to focus on our reasons for being here on earth and igniting our "exuberance for God and life" (how *The Message* speaks of joy).

As I see it:

---

[18] I wrote this from memory, but it was based on the Baltimore Catechism I, Lesson 01. *See References at the back of the book.

- To Know God means to relate to God intimately based on frequent conversations and time in His presence and His Word.

- To Love God means to abide in God and God in you. Abiding is easily understood using the metaphor of Jesus as the vine, His followers as the branches, and the Father as the vine grower. The branches don't go off and act independently, doing whatever they decide. They remain connected, and the vine grower prunes them during the right season.

- To Serve God requires loving Him and aligning your life with what God wills. That also includes loving your neighbor, and showing compassion, respect, and love for yourself and others. You also align your interior and exterior beliefs, thoughts, feelings, and behaviors so they match, demonstrating honesty and integrity. When you are aligned with God, your inner self, and others, you bear good fruit with the divine assistance of the Holy Spirit, thus serving God.

The second half may be your ideal opportunity to share your joy and wisdom with others, perhaps by proclaiming more than ever what God has done for you.

Radiating inner joy and the transforming power of the Holy Spirit has a sunbeam effect. God brings about or allows the circumstances that require change, resulting in divine order. Let your faith rest in the assurance that nothing escapes His notice, and when you call for help, God is there to give wisdom and direction. "Call to Me, and I will answer you and show you great and mighty things, which you do not know (Jeremiah 33:3).

> Joyful is the person who finds wisdom, the one who gains understanding. For wisdom is more profitable than silver ... nothing you desire can compare with her. She offers you long life ... She will guide you down delightful paths; all her ways are satisfying. Wisdom is a tree of life to those who embrace her; happy are those who hold her tightly. ~Proverbs 3:13-18

Finding My REAL Self

After my conversion experience thirty-five years ago, I was well-meaning but still constantly striving. I yearned to be a good and upright person (in all my roles, including daughter, student, real estate broker, serial home renovator, lawyer, wife, mother, grandmother, ministry volunteer, and speaker). That's a full load of striving! Underneath external appearances, I was a self-protective over-doer trying to better myself and earn approval. I believed I was not good enough, seriously flawed, and in need of constant improvement.

Since 1992 when I read Julia Cameron's *The Artist's Way*, I have loved this quote about the uniqueness of each person God created:

> "There is a vitality, a life force, a quickening that is translated through you into action, and there is only one of you in all time, this expression is unique, and if you block it, it will never exist through any other medium; and be lost. The world will not have it. It is not your business to determine how good it is, not how it compares with other expression. It is your

business to keep it yours clearly and directly, to keep the channel open."
~Martha Graham[19]

Sadly, I didn't take that to heart for decades. I kept myself busy with hours of prayer and journaling, reading inspirational books, and enrolling in self-improvement or spiritual development programs. Even though I was comfortable with public speaking or in a courtroom, I struggled to speak up freely in my personal life and to shed old behaviors and ways of thinking.

Too often, I'd criticize, judge, complain, or give unsolicited advice. I timidly held back in gatherings, feeling like hiding when I was ill at ease, and too often quiet in situations that called for full and honest expression. In retrospect, those behaviors stopped me from being my most authentic self and the person God created me to be—a confident, fearless, faith-filled woman, unconcerned about other people's opinions. If only I could stop seeking people's approval and always trying to do things "right," I hoped and wished I'd finally focus on the

---

[19] Goodreads, Martha Graham>Quotes>Quotable Quote, https://www.goodreads.com/quotes/680327-there-is-a-vitality-a-life-force-a-quickening-that, accessed September 30 2024.

heart and do things out of love, surrender, faith, and trust in God.

Of course, my spirit and soul weren't stagnant all those years, nor were my mind and body. Beginning with my come-to-Jesus-and-baptism-in-the-Holy-Spirit surprise, I learned from the good, the bad, and downright ugly life experiences. During a pilgrimage to the Holy Land, I sobbed at Gethsemane, feeling Jesus' suffering on my account, realizing that Jesus' agony wasn't only dread of the physical suffering he'd face. What seemed to me heavier still was His understanding of how many people would not believe or embrace what He did to redeem them.

Pastors along my way acknowledged gratitude for my gifts and willingness to serve, which built up my spirit perhaps, but more likely, my ego. A few years later, our family went through major upheaval with Ryan's teenage pregnancy and learning about an abusive situation beforehand, which led to our having two teens and a toddler-grandchild at home. Further challenges and estrangements followed when the teens were young adults and moved out.

Those experiences, between 2004 and 2013, propelled me to attend a Benedictine School for

Charismatic Spiritual Directors and training in Christian Healing Ministries with Francis and Judith MacNutt. I also published my first book, *Reap As You Sew: Spirit at Work in Quiltmaking*.

Finally, family estrangement led me to seek help, healing, and a way through the challenges. I learned how to forgive. To serve others, I then underwent two kinds of training and became radically dedicated to healing and deliverance prayer ministry. I learned how to draw on the power of the Holy Spirit and the Holy Name of Jesus to identify and release emotional residue and to pray for the casting out of unclean spirits, generational curses, unholy vows, and soul ties. I learned how to listen, love, and pray for others.

Until that training, and even for some time afterward, before the pandemic, I didn't recognize the big lies preventing me from seeing Truth. I believed that love must be earned. But the truth is that love is a free gift from God and from people, to the best of their imperfect abilities. I believed that perfection was achievable by human beings on earth. It is not. The word translated as "perfect" in Matthew 5:38 makes more sense to me in the Amplified Bible: "You, therefore, will be perfect [growing into spiritual maturity both in mind and character, actively integrating godly values into your daily life], as your heavenly Father is perfect."[20]

Shortly before the pandemic began, I enrolled in an online course Debrena Jackson Gandy designed to help women she described as "Rippin' and Runnin', Efforting, Busy, Overdoing, and Overwhelmed." The course helped participants become "Juicy Women." I have participated in online programs led by Debrena for five years, continuously digging deeper, doing more inner work, and elevating our visions, consciousness, and intentions among a cohort of strong women of faith.

During 2022-2023, I wrote a twice-as-long forerunner of this book. Then I realized I had relied too much on myself, so I pulled it back from the publisher and started over, yielding to more guidance from the Holy Spirit. A clear sign that the book was too much me, and too little Spirit, is that it was really difficult to complete, with a college-like all-nighter near the end. That is *not* being yoked to

---

[20] See https://biblehub.com/amp/matthew/5.htm, accessed October 8, 2024; see also Lockman Foundation, AMPLIFIED BIBLE, https://www.lockman.org/amplified/, accessed October 8, 2024. *Continued in References at the back of the book.

Jesus, because His yoke is easy, and my burden wasn't light (*cf.* Matthew 11:30). Now this is one book in what the Spirit tells me will be part of a series of shorter books that the Holy Spirit will direct. I am to be "a priestly pen in the hands of the Author of life," as my Christian writing mentors C.J. and Shelley Hitz say!

Even after that realization, however, I persisted in trying to do too much, and I knew it! I knew from chapter 15 of the Gospel of John that I was attached to Jesus (the Vine) and needed pruning. I clipped away tiny shoots, but not enough.

When you prune a fruit tree, you remove branches that interfere with heartier branches. Spiritually, that was a call to eliminate whatever interfered with aligning myself with God's will, abiding in Him, and heeding His directions. You also prune dead branches. From a biblical perspective, that meant the attitudes and behaviors of my sinful nature had to go, which at the time included feeling like a victim of emotional abuse. I had to do inner work and realize I could speak the truth in love and decide to no longer allow the abuse. Another kind of fruit tree pruning is removing unproductive suckers. That meant I needed to remove my chronic busyness—

easier said than done—and avoid situations where noise and crowds distract my focus away from my Psalm 46:10 enjoyment of "being still and knowing that [God is] God."

I host a monthly podcast on audio channels and YouTube to promote my website and prepare for book launches. As a milestone birthday approached, a "Juicy" friend suggested a special birthday episode for my podcast. She was also the head of my new tech team, and she had expressed concern about how much effort editing the podcast would require. Aiming to please my family, my audience, and the new tech team, I fell back into my old, compulsive striving for excellence. I decided (without God's input) to create the podcast on new software that I thought I could edit myself.

I invested a week of long, unyoked, self-reliant days trying to complete that task, and when I submitted the files to the tech team, I learned they were in a format they couldn't work with. I spent another day trying to recreate the video on my familiar platform, and I still wanted to include twenty photo memories. I couldn't get those files uploaded correctly. At that point, I focused on how much time I'd put into previous podcasts and how much that had interfered with writing, which is what God has specifically instructed me to make my priority.

I crashed.

In utter despair and exhaustion, I decided not to do any more podcasts. The next day, I took the matter to prayer and to a trusted coach, focusing on mindset, self-image, and dying to self. I saw that I'd allowed people-pleasing, conforming to worldly values, and false beliefs to frustrate me, keep me busy, distracted, and unavailable for the joy I could be embracing all around me. I knew I had to prune that striving.

The timing was just right for radical change. I had some lifework to do for a class with Debrena: to handwrite my vision for the next 90 days. I knew I wanted to live with greater ease, yoked to Jesus (Matthew 11:30). I wanted to take responsibility for cooperating with the Holy Spirit and not feel like a victim! I was already focusing on my self-care, and I wanted to reinforce a way of life to optimize my energy—physically, spiritually, mentally, and emotionally.

As part of my pruning, I planned to clear out emotional and spiritual clutter. I'd start the new epoch by transforming my mind rather than conforming to external, worldly expectations. I'd listen, love, and speak the truth in love. I'd be obedient to God and not self-reliant. I'd stop complaining, taking offense, and judging, and I'd extinguish negativity. I'd honor my sacred self-care, knowing my body is a temple of the Holy Spirit, and self-love honors God in me (1 Corinthians 6:19-20). I'd stop faking, suppressing, stuffing, and avoiding the authentic expression of the REAL me. I would act knowing that, set free in Christ, I get to choose to surrender and always be available to Him—however much Quiet Time I need to get back in the spiritual groove when I am weak and need an infusion of God's strength.

You know what helped me the most? The work I'd done on writing this book. Jesus wanted me to take into my life all I wrote about! I repented and started anew ... once again. Freed, my spirit went into action, re-igniting a fire within. That's the radiating light of joy I want to bring wherever I go, so help me, God!

Help me God surely did! He's brought me to complete this book and to draft another one in the series. No longer located near a healing and deliverance team, He led me to start an online group that has transformed the lives of mature believers through greater trust, surrender, connection, and joy—a program I'll offer online again because it was so life-changing. Together, believers have come to understand and are living out many of the concepts presented in this book. Praise be to God!

PRAYER

Praise You, Jesus, that I am never alone for You are Emmanuel, God-with-us! I give You thanks in all circumstances as I reflect on what I've lived through. Please show me how You worked everything together for my temporal and/or eternal good. I'm grateful for the blessings of this season of my life and I look forward with hope to what You have for me in coming seasons. Thank You for the elder role models in The Bible. I offer You myself to be a role model for others as I imitate You, walk by the Spirit, and become the genuine, free person the Creator always intended me to be, with Your grace!

REFLECTION QUESTIONS
(For Individual Use or with a Small Group)

1. What opportunities do you participate in where you can speak confidentially with faith-filled peers? Would you like to share surprises, challenges, blessings, and perhaps whether you'd want to return to your younger years?

2. How does the statement "All my time is FREE time" strike you?

3. What experiences of yours support the ideas that nothing is wasted with God, that He works all things for good, and that gray hair is a crown of glory for godly living?

4. Which of the nine days of the Surrender Prayer touch your heart as most challenging? Are you willing to pray that for nine days or longer?

5. Ask God what season you're in. Listen and write down what you hear. Follow up with questions until you sense what God wants you to know. It's better to focus on the final

outcome or big picture, rather than a How or Why question.

Chapter 4
What Impedes Rejoicing and Letting Your Light Shine?

Impediments to joy may relate to your body, mind, soul, spirit, or circumstances. You can deal with challenging circumstances better when you're walking in the Spirit, being the REAL You, and allowing the Lord to guide and direct you. The Holy Spirit within will enliven you with good fruit including love, peace, patience, joy, and faithfulness.

If you don't experience joy, let's explore why not. For joy is in our nature as creatures in God's own image. Let's break down some of the impediments to radiating joy, identify the underlying problem, and consider helpful responses.

Do You Need a Faith Booster?

Faith brings joy, but what is faith? "Though you have not seen him, you love him. Though you do not now see him, you believe in him and rejoice with joy that is inexpressible and filled with glory, obtaining the outcome of your faith, the salvation of your souls" (1 Peter 1:8-9 ESV).

Most of the Christian faithful would say the ultimate joy is eternal life. But if eternal joy seems unreal or too far off to uplift you regularly, maybe deep down you believe you're already assured of entry into Heaven regardless of your beliefs and whether you yield to God's will. Perhaps you hold onto the idea that a loving God would never condemn anyone. Or you have no hope of deserving, meriting, or getting into Heaven (if it even exists).

We are meant to be truly glad, knowing that wonderful joy lies ahead, even though we must endure many trials for a little while (the remaining duration of our temporary life on earth)—trials that will show the genuineness of our faith, which is tested as fire tests and purifies gold (1 Peter 1:6 ESV). The testing is intended to bolster our endurance, because when our faith remains strong through adversity, it brings heavenly rewards on the last day (Peter 1:7 ESV). If you have the hope of joyful eternal life, definitely hang onto it.

If you lack faith, however, the prospect of Heavenly joy won't motivate or give you hope. A well-known Bethel Church leader, Bill Johnson, preaches, "Any area of our lives for which we have no hope is under the influence of a lie."[21] The "father of lies" is our spiritual adversary, the evil deceiver, Satan (John 8:44). If you're without faith (even temporarily), the devil has you where he wants you, and God wants you to receive a fresh infusion of faith, however, that may come to pass.

My late spiritual director, Abbot David Gereats, O.S.B., used to say that God wants to get our attention to draw us into a loving relationship with Him. If He doesn't get it with a tap on our shoulder, a disciple's witness, or an outstanding sunrise, He may just have to let you get hit with a hard knock.

---

[21] Bill Johnson, Facebook, July 27, 2015, https://www.facebook.com/BillJohnsonMinistries/photos/any-area-of-our-lives-for-which-we-have-no-hope-is-under-the-influence-of-a-lie-/, accessed October 10, 2024. Bill Johnson is Senior Leader at Bethel Church in Redding, California.

Romans 5, verses 1 and 2, emphasize the role of faith in our lives and the privilege we enjoy as Christian disciples, primarily because we have believed and trusted what we could not see with our own eyes. We can confidently and joyfully look forward to Heaven, where we'll share God's glory. We enter by faith into what God's always wanted to do for us: set us in a loving relationship with Him and make us fit for Him! Then "we have it all together with God" because of Jesus, and we discover that God's already made a way and thrown open His door to us, leading us to express our joy, rejoicing and shouting our praise. (Romans 5:1-2 *The Message*).

If you pray for a new infusion or an increase in faith, that's certainly a prayer aligned with God's will, and if you mean it and believe He can deliver on your request, it will be granted. When Jesus speaks of the absurdity of an earthly father who, if a son asks for a fish or an egg, will give him a snake or a scorpion instead, He was making this point: "How much more will your Father in heaven give the Holy Spirit to those who ask Him!" (Luke 11:11-12).

And great faith is not required. If you can say with the faith of a humble leper, "If Jesus wills it, he can make us clean," then His will is all that's necessary (see Matthew 8:2). When the apostles asked Jesus to increase their faith, He replied, "If you have faith as small as a mustard seed, you can say to this mulberry tree, 'Be uprooted and planted in the sea,' and it will obey you'" (Luke 17:5-6).

In the story of the father with the son possessed by an impure spirit in Mark 9:17-29, the father explains the situation and says to Jesus, "...if you can do anything, take pity on us and help us."

"'If you can'?" said Jesus. "Everything is possible for one who believes."

Immediately the boy's father exclaimed, "I do believe; help me overcome my unbelief!" That prayer was granted, along with the boy's deliverance.

How Can Anyone Stay Joyful and Rejoice Always?

Saint Paul tells us the kind of thoughts we're supposed to have—thoughts that align with living in joy all the time! He says not to be anxious about anything (Philippians 3:6). Think instead about these things: "whatever is true, whatever is noble, whatever is right, whatever is pure, whatever is lovely, whatever is admirable—if anything is excellent or praiseworthy—think about such things" (Philippians 4:8). Saint Paul says joy and spiritually encouraged thoughts will guard both your heart and your mind in Christ Jesus, bringing you amazing peace (Philippians 4:7-8). That promise is appealing, but compliance may seem impossible.

The New Testament instructs Christians in twenty-four different verses to rejoice. To rejoice is an active, conscious response: to feel or show triumphant elation or jubilation; to enjoy something immensely; to engage in joyous celebration; or to delight.[22] Saint Paul exhorted the Philippians to "Rejoice in the Lord always." He says this twice in Philippians 4:4, and he repeats it in his First Letter to the Thessalonians (1 Thessalonians 5:16). And, yes, Saint Paul's message is that we are even to rejoice in our sufferings or persecution, as Peter, Paul, Matthew, and Luke all wrote.

---

[22] WordHippo App, info@wordhippo.com, "What is another word for rejoice," accessed September 4, 2024.

What do you think about regularly? The last episode's cliffhanger and the crazy characters on a show you're binge-watching? How someone hurt or judged you? How lousy the weather is or the inconvenience of long lines at the DMV or a package arriving late? Do you worry about your adult children, grandkids, or aging relatives? How much conversation involves complaining about health issues when you're with peers or older folks?

On the other hand, there are times you probably delight in special settings, creativity, or moments of blessed connection that might start out or contain a bit of earthly happiness, but they can also become memories of joy, like holy moments that stay with us for years or a lifetime.

We shouldn't be too dualistic (that is, stuck in black-and-white thinking) about what is spiritual and what is earthly. When God provides these things for us, why not rejoice and give thanks? Although they may be physical, God's provision is a blessing. He has made each day for us to rejoice in and be glad (Psalm 118:24). Every good and perfect gift comes from God (James 1:17).

God isn't a curmudgeon! "Rejoice always" means all ways! Whatever is good, excellent, praiseworthy, and beautiful includes events, scenery, creativity, and other good things that happen in our earthly lives. Just before His public ministry began, Jesus, His friends, and His mother attended a wedding feast (typically in that era, a week-long celebration). Jesus did His first glorious sign there, and His disciples came to believe in Him (John 2:1-11).

He acknowledges in various passages that in the presence of a bridegroom, one doesn't fast (see Matthew 9:14-15, Mark 2:19). There was probably dancing, toasting the couple, telling fun stories, and sharing a good time. And plenty of wine was consumed—so much that Jesus' mother implored Him to do something about it when the six stone water jars ran empty, and Jesus, with only a sentence, turned water into fine wine (see John 2:6). O, Joy!

In Matthew, chapter 6, Jesus speaks of prayer, fasting, and almsgiving and teaches His disciples the Lord's Prayer. During that teaching, He says we're not to babble on about all we want or need, nor should we store up earthly treasures or try to serve both God and money. We must protect our eyes (presumably all our entryways) from darkness.

Jesus also mentions worries that pagans have about what to eat, drink, or wear. As His children, we are not to worry because God loves us and knows what we need. He reassures us and gives us an amazing promise related to some of those very down-to-earth things when He says, "Seek first his kingdom and his righteousness, and all these things will be given to you as well" (Matthew 6:33)—especially if you've surrendered fully and asked Jesus to take care of everything!

Is the Current Season of Your Life Presenting Age-Related Impediments to Joy?

Are you tempted to give up because you're feeling tired, weary, or too old to be useful? The Bible says that even in old age, godly people will flourish, and even in old age they will still produce fruit, remaining vital and green (Psalms 92:14 NLT). Galatians 6:9 says: "And let us not grow weary while doing good, for in due season we shall reap if we do not lose heart."

However, some older women may not have adjusted to the ways in which they can bear fruit in this period of life. The variety of fruit they're to bear may change over time. God knows all our strengths, gifts, weaknesses, and limitations. Therefore, God will only ask of us what He already knows we're capable of. He never expects us to carry out the assignment on our own, in our own strength. Let's reframe our perspective, if necessary.

For example, I connected with an author who is close to Jesus and the Holy Spirit and specializes in helping Christians through grief (along with other kinds of healing work). I love her line, "I'm not retired, I'm re-fired!"[23]

Though I never met her, I knew from others of a woman named Shirley who was quite a prayer warrior. She was close to death from cancer, and she knew it. Nevertheless, Shirley interceded for me at the request of her long-time prayer partner, who led a prayer session at which I received healing prayer. Although Shirley didn't attend my prayer session in person, she interceded from her home,

---

[23] Author's personal conversation on July 31, 2024, with Debbie Jordan, author of *Journey through Grief.*

and that day the Lord blessed me with a real breakthrough in inner healing.

A couple of months later, Shirley went home to the Lord, and some months after that, she showed up as a character in one of my dreams. I sensed her symbolizing the importance of continuing to bear good fruit all our days, as the Spirit confirmed Shirley's role in the healing I experienced.

The morning after my dream about Shirley, I had my first appointment with a spiritual director for whom I had waited months to be accepted as one of her regular directees. I received another confirmation about Shirley's role in my life upon learning the spiritual director had given me the spot that had belonged to Shirley. In physical pain and weakness, without family around her, Shirley had continued to bear good fruit.

Poor sleep can be harmful at any age, but it tends to afflict seniors more than younger people (except those with babies or maybe teenagers out late at night). I have had a lot of experience with insomnia: former difficulty falling asleep. What we think or fret about at night is usually the past or the future, not the present (except for thinking about not being asleep). God designed us to live in the present and in His presence, even or especially in bed.

Any striving about performance that keeps us awake has its roots in identity issues, usually our identity as human DOings rather than on our BEing beloved daughters of the King. Jesus has repeatedly told me to rest, reminding me I don't have to do anything but love from the heart! After receiving healing prayer, I've had a new lease on falling asleep and staying asleep until the Lord calls me to get up.

If you expect to be as active and energetic in your eighties as you were in your fifties, or anywhere in between, you may need to take your expectations to the Lord for a deep, conversational time of prayer. Surrender to Him, be in relationship with the three persons of the Trinity, and be open to divine appointments and specific assignments. Be available to God and when He calls your name, respond like Isaiah, "Here I am. Send me" (Isaiah 6:8)!

In terms of changing how we serve, we might ask: Is God calling us to recognize that our yearnings will serve us and others in the process of becoming who God calls us to be? Remember, God delights in giving us the desires of our heart, because He put them there, and He may have set up the circumstances and opportunities by which they developed in us (Psalm 21:2, *cf.* Deuteronomy 2:7, 1 John 3:2).

F.E.A.R. Means Full Expression Avoided and Resisted

A fear that many women in our generation have can be called "F.E.A.R. – Full Expression Avoided and Resisted," a term coined by Debrena Jackson Gandy. It refers to all the ways we hold back from saying what we really think, feel, believe, need, or want, because we grew up in a culture and time where children and women were to be seen and not heard, subservient to men or others, non-confrontational, and just "nice."

Here are some of the common things kids heard growing up that engender the development of the false self and lead many women to F.E.A.R:

- What will people think?
- Children are to be seen and not heard.
- Cut the histrionics!
- If you can't put on a happy face, go to your room.

- Stop crying or I'll give you something to cry about!
- Shame on you.
- You should be ashamed of yourself.
- Don't air your dirty laundry.
- What happens at home stays at home.
- This is a secret. Don't tell anyone.
- If you can't say something nice, don't say anything at all.
- Actions speak louder than words.
- You'll never amount to anything.

What can we do about these early messages? Remember, our F.E.A.R. doesn't stand a chance when we stand firm in the love of God.

Most women have internalized a slew of inhibiting messages as kids that may still silence them until they complete some healing work, maybe some deliverance, and practice better forms of communication. Believing you have to be "nice," and forcing yourself to say "yes" when everything in you wants to say "no," often leads to resentment and letting the false self take over. It's also not aligned with the spiritual principles of honesty and integrity.

"Niceness" can be a real trap, as Dr. Aziz Gazipura teaches in his books and conferences that train people to have more confidence and communicate with kindness rather than conforming to societal niceness.[24] Just reading the titles of these two books provides a lot to ponder:

- *Not Nice: Stop People Pleasing, Staying Silent, & Feeling Guilty—And Start Speaking Up, Saying No, Asking Boldly, and Unapologetically Being Yourself* (2017); and
- *Less Nice, More You: Stop Hiding & Become the Most Bold, Authentic Version of You Now* (2023).

Although not Christian books, the *Less Nice* book was insightful and helpful for me.

Ladies, the Creator made us wonderfully complex (Psalm 139:14 NLT). We are God's workmanship, here to do what He prepared in advance—so we must express our voices, our uniqueness, and our

---

[24] See Dr. Aziz Gazipura's Author Page on Amazon.com, https://www.amazon.com/stor Hisziz-Gazipura/author/B00D0U4AMQ, accessed October 6, 2024, and his books *Not Nice: Stop People Pleasing, Staying Silent, & Feeling Guilty—And Start Speaking Up Saying No, Asking Boldly, and Unapologetically Being Yourself (2017)* and *Less Nice, More You: Stop Hiding & Become the Most Bold, Authentic Version of You Now (2023)*.

gifts (See Ephesians 2:10). For years, stifling my self-expression stifled my joy! Aim first for progress, not perfection. Do not let the world control you, for "If you belonged to the world, it would love you as its own.

As it is, you do not belong to the world, but I [the Lord] have chosen you out of the world. That is why the world hates you" (John 15:19). Instead, "Do not be conformed to this world, but be transformed by the renewal of your mind, that by testing you may discern what is the will of God, what is good and acceptable and perfect" (Romans 12:2 ESV).

How Are We Supposed to Face Trials?

Earlier I referred to James, chapter one, about trials that test our faith and perseverance and about presenting petitions to God without doubt. Please bear with me as I quote it again in the context of how to face trials.

> "Consider it pure joy, my brothers and sisters, whenever you face trials of many kinds, because you know that the testing of your faith produces perseverance. Let

perseverance finish its work so that you may be mature and complete, not lacking anything" (James 1:2-4).

When using *Lectio Divina* with that passage: "not lacking anything" jumps out at me. Does this mean facing trials as joy leads to not lacking time, energy, money, friends, book content, podcast ability, ideas, or anything else? "Whenever" jumps out at me, too. "Whenever" means every time there's a trial. To "persevere" means to continue to press through a difficult time, counting on the Lord to give you the strength, ingenuity, or other means to succeed. And "endurance" signifies a long time, involving hanging on for as long as it takes, maybe indefinitely, and appreciating and being grateful for the fruits of the process: maturity and completion! Grace, patience, faith, and trust.

Saint Paul also tells us to rejoice when we run into sufferings or trials because they lead us to hope, and hope doesn't disappoint us, because God's love has been poured into our hearts through the Holy Spirit who was given to us (Romans 5:5 WEBC).

Developing Spiritual Poise

It helps to face all circumstances with spiritual poise, which I believe is a fantastic approach to radiant joy!

Spiritual poise is graciousness, confidence, humility, and elegance when circumstances get stirred up, and you remain in faith, relaxed, compassionate, unflustered, and responsive rather than reactive.

"Humility" is when you keep allowing God to use you as a vessel or instrument—yielded and surrendered (as opposed to having an overgrown ego).

A mark of humility is to put forward ASKS and call on God for guidance and direction. Here's to learning these responses, unswayed from their importance by success in money, power, fame, or visibility.[25] (You might just nickname Spiritual Poise "cool, calm, and collected," which is easier to remember, as long as you remember it stands for a grace-filled response.)

When it comes to remaining attached to the vine and living righteously with spiritual poise, the two most important commandments are to love God with all your heart, soul, mind, and strength (Mark 12:30) and to love one another as Jesus has loved us (John 15:11-12). An aspect less emphasized, especially to women who grew up in the fifties and sixties, is to love others the same way you love yourself (Luke 10:27), with the understanding that loving yourself is neither optional nor selfish. Jesus asks us to lay down our lives for Him (John 13:38)— that is, die to your selfish or worldly desires (1 John 2:16)—but that doesn't mean that loving yourself is selfish.

Your body is a temple of the living God, and you are God's wonderfully made "very good" creation (2 Corinthians 6:16, Psalm 139:17, Genesis 1:31). Self-

---

[25] I learned these (and much more) from Debrena Jackson Gandy, who has been a model of spiritual poise through life's ups and downs. See www.milliondollarmentor.net.

loathing, self-neglect, and streams of negative self-talk are ungodly "unclean" spirits, and spiritual warfare and inner healing can help you kick them out of your life.

The Challenge of Thinking Like Jesus

In the second half of my life, I began to believe that God gave me an abundant life and that I am capable of cooperating with God, who desires to cooperate because of my weaknesses and His strength! So, I smiled and said one day, and then over and over to keep reaffirming these thoughts: "Yes, Lord, I'm yours and I'm ready. I am more than enough because in my weakness I am made strong, and I am equipped and qualified for what you call me to do 'through Christ who strengthens me.' Thank you, Jesus, that you have already won my spiritual battles."[26]

But humility and obedience are real challenges!

If I had been humble and obedient from the start, this book would have been well written and

---

[26] The thoughts are based on 2 Corinthians 12:10, Ephesians 2:10, Philippians 4:13 (ESV), and 1 Corinthians 15:57 (ESV).

published long ago, instead of being the third version of what's been in the works for over two years. And if I'd been humbly yielded to God's will and obeyed for forty or fifty years already, perhaps my whole family might be on fire for Jesus. I can't even imagine what else might have been different in my relationships, my life, in everything. I am not going back into the past in regret. It was all used for good in the long run. I now see that humility and surrendering to God's will like a dependent child in my Abba Father's arms, as Saint Thérèse put it, and praying to put on the mind of Christ—I see these as the keys to life in Christ. I used to think about not trying to be in control, but a better reframe is: "Now is the time to walk in the Spirit, surrender and be the REAL me, radiating the joy of the Lord!"

To help us think like Jesus, we can use the Word to discern the thoughts and intents of hearts. We can stand fearless in the face of adversity. The Lord will give us the wisdom necessary to lead us out of any predicament. We need to bring every thought captive to the obedience of Christ (2 Corinthians 10:5). We must not listen to ungodly voices but rather, align our actions with the Word of God.

We need to commit to honesty and integrity, which entails keeping our word to God, others, and ourselves, so as not to be hypocrites (Matthew 23:13-22). Since 2020, I've participated in groups of 25 to 45 women of faith who held each other accountable for integrity and honesty. We had to learn what that meant, and then we had to notice when we did or did not act accordingly. We grew so much by focusing on keeping our promises and commitments and being truthful that we bonded as a group and experienced countless individual breakthroughs in multiple areas of our lives.

To think like Jesus, we need to know Jesus. "Be still and know that I am God," Psalm 46:10 exhorts us. Know His Word. Recall Chapter One about Jesus, Joy, and Abiding. Revisit Chapter Two about imitating Jesus and putting on the Mind of Christ. Connect with the Holy Spirit like Chapter 5 outlines, because the Holy Spirit reveals Jesus and inspired the Word of God. Try different prayer approaches, such as those offered in Chapter 6, and discover those that help you enter two-way conversations with the Lord.

Jesus was not a people-pleaser seeking approval. He was a radical doing His Father's will. He overturned tables, and He didn't let the religious leaders of the time intimidate Him or get Him to back down. He didn't give Pontius Pilate the answers he sought. And much more. So, people-pleasing is not an aspect of putting on the Mind of Christ.

Life is exhausting when you try to please everyone, an attitude that leads you to make choices based on approval-seeking or pleasing others rather than pleasing God and seeking and carrying out His will. A prayer by Thomas Merton asks for the grace of divine respect: " ... I believe that the desire to please you does in fact please you. And I hope I have that desire in all that I am doing. I hope that I will never do anything apart from that desire. ... I will not fear, for you are ever with me, and you will never leave me to face my perils alone."[27]

Poor King Herod! In the Gospel passage in Matthew 14:1-12, he seems conflicted at every turn. Herod wants to kill John the Baptist but is afraid of the people who revere John as a prophet. He is delighted by Salome's dance, but after his intemperate promise, the king is distressed that she demands John's beheading. He feels caught when his public oath must be kept because his guests

---

[27] *See* Sr. Kathleen Hughes, RSCJ, *Give Us This Day,* August 3, 2024, Reflection, "Divine Respect"

overheard the promise he made. Herod seems entirely paralyzed by the opinions of others.[28]

The root of people-pleasing is a lie or a collection of lies. In Herod's case, a lie was: I must keep my word given in front of others regardless of the wrong that will ensue. For many others, lies might include: I must prove my worth. I must earn love. I will receive love if I just do what makes others happy. Love is out of my reach. Loving myself is selfish. What I have to say is unimportant. My wants and desires are self-centered. If I love someone, I'll end up hurt. Pleasing people avoids rejection.

Do Any Old Beliefs Limit You?

As a child, my image of God the Father resembled that of an old, strict, school principal, a white-bearded man in the sky with a blackboard. He constantly monitored me and everyone else and recorded a chalk mark every time He saw me sin. If I messed up, the punishment could be Purgatory or Hell.

My earthly father was a humorous, honorable, caring young man who traveled for business most

---

[28] *Id.*

weekdays. When in town, he would unwind after work by reading, undisturbed in the off-limits-to-kids living room. He and Mom ate dinner separately from the kids, except on Sundays. Sunday nights, I loved sitting next to Dad at our table for seven; he would favor me with second helpings.

He and Mom were perfectionists, doing their best as parents by pointing out our mistakes so we could learn to excel. I interpreted their pointers to mean I wasn't good enough. I continuously strove to raise my performance levels, trying to earn approval. If I messed up, I'd be grounded, which felt, if not like Hell, at least like Purgatory.

I didn't experience the Truth in either case. From an earthly perspective, I succeeded, though spiritually, I had a lot to learn. Father God, Mom, and Dad all love me deeply and always have! I know nothing about your parents. I do, however, understand about our shared Father.

God created us in love, with a purposeful plan.

He sent His only begotten Son (our Heavenly Brother) to redeem us and show us how to live in the glorious freedom and the complete joy of beloved children of the Most High. This almighty, ever-loving Father revealed His plan and purpose throughout Scripture, in signs and wonders, and in the prayer Jesus taught us.

But living in the past or regret is not what the Lord wants for us. Focusing on our inadequacies or failures takes our minds and hearts off the better part, sitting at the feet of Jesus like Mary of Bethany (Luke 10:42 ESV). God wants us living in His presence, fullness, and joy—abiding with Him, yoked to Him, being the holy temple of the Spirit— embracing the new creation we are, repenting and receiving God's mercy rather than lamenting what our sinful nature thought or did.

We are not our sin. That's not our identity. Saint Paul is a perfect example of struggling with a sinful nature and yet fulfilling a Kingdom assignment of monumental proportions, still blessing millions or billions of Christians who read the New Testament. And his past? He persecuted Christians! (Acts 22:7).

Once lies are identified, there's a process for ascertaining the truth, releasing the unhealthy feelings, and embracing or embodying the truth that sets you free. This is part of a process often called "Inner Work."

Inner Work is Essential to Live Free as the REAL You

The Harvard Law School faculty recently shared stories and tips for managing mental health and reducing stress. Professor Dehlia Umumma, faculty director of the school's Criminal Justice Institute, said she'd tell her younger self that it's okay to be all of the REAL you unapologetically, with an appreciation of aspects of your identity, explaining that she holds near and dear to her heart that she is Black, a woman, an immigrant, and a Christian.

Growing up, she was taught not to take time to process trauma, but she now knows the importance of being present in the moment and processing pain. "I'm learning to pause, process the trauma, process the pain, process the hurt because I realize that if I don't, unresolved trauma and pain and hurt has a way of manifesting itself in ways that are unhealthy and at inopportune times."[29]

I've mentioned that I have served in healing and deliverance ministry for over a decade, helping people conquer trauma and darkness that plagued them since their childhoods or early adulthood years and drove them into unhealthy or unholy patterns of thinking and behaving. But it needn't reach the level of "trauma" to seek ministry.

I have also been the one prayed for in ministry sessions over the years. Forgiving and inner healing are not usually "one and done" because it's as if we're peeling an onion. When the outer layers are removed, more layers remain so we must go deeper and deeper. That's a reason healing processes merit periodic engagement.

You now know I tried to earn love by constantly striving to prove myself worthy. My parents meant well, but to me, they seemed overly critical. The truth that it took me years to learn is that there were

---

[29] Email from The Harvard Gazette to an email list, October 16, 2024, including an article by Christine Perkins, Harvard Law Today - Campus & Community, "Give yourself grace," October 3, 2024,

only three incidents when their words affected me enough to trigger the formation of a lie. Three remarks in seventeen years of living at home! Being a nearly perfect parent is not just challenging but, I believe, impossible!

Our kids also thought I was too critical. If I'd had a different upbringing, I might have been more accustomed to speaking up, with the courage to communicate with more integrity and honesty, not just with our kids, but with everyone. In a 2022 ministry session, we cracked open generational issues head-on, including my parents and their parents. We peeled away many layers and went deep to find the roots of my pain. That part of the prayer session was valuable, but not as transformative as what happened next.

Just as the session was ending, the Holy Spirit released an astonishing twenty-year-old memory into my awareness. The setting was a formal dinner with my husband Toby's business colleagues and their wives, at which I uncharacteristically fully expressed my concern. I told his boss Joe that Toby's constant travel to Asia was hurting our family. A war veteran, Joe's response to me included a threat to kill anyone who questioned his leadership.

I was devastated by what he said and how aggressively he said it. I escaped to the Ladies' Room to cry. The others at the dinner were stunned, but nothing changed with Toby's travel schedule. I became bitter and resentful and harbored ill will (and, as the Spirit revealed during the session, hatred) towards Joe.

I repented of disparaging and focusing on the weaknesses of others, criticizing and judging them. In Jesus' name, I forgave Joe, my parents, and myself for all our mistaken ways and harsh words. The critical spirit was cast out, along with judging and discouragement. I was delivered from those "Joe" issues and the generational patterns, including seeking the approval of others, related spirits, and guilt! I felt free of the bondage of believing others have power over me when the truth is that I have free will and the power of choice (knowing, through the study of biblical principles, that choices have consequences).

I put my family members into the Lord's hands, acknowledging that I'm not responsible for their choices or outcomes, and I'm not in control of their lives (nor should I be). We broke unhealthy codependency soul ties. What sobs and moans poured out in that session! (Admittedly, some of these have to be cast out more that once.)

Not long afterward, I was preparing to speak at an Unbound conference on "Ministering to Others in Partnership with the Holy Spirit."[30] While tweaking my PowerPoint presentation, I received a huge insight. I had taken on a victim spirit from the incident with Joe. I had felt powerless and abused. My finally speaking truth to someone with power felt like it backfired.

From that time forward, I felt like a victim of my husband's job, and as insights continued on my drive home from the conference, I saw what that victim spirit had done. I apologized to Toby for having been angry and resentful of how much he was away, and how those feelings had overflowed into my parenting because, out of self-pity, I'd labeled myself a "*de facto* single parent."

I wasn't really a bad mom; I was a mom who was broken and unhealed. What hurt our family's peace and harmony was not Toby's travel; it was my

---

[30] The event was sponsored by the Albuquerque Catholic Charismatic Center Unbound Team.

resentment and frustrated helplessness over a situation I believed was unalterable.

Since that healing, Toby and I have grown much closer in our marriage, and I have been able to reconcile beautifully with one of our kids who had previously been lost to me. I can also now more easily discern the victim spirit in others and help them get over it.

Forgiveness and Emotional Release

My transformational coaching and spiritual direction programs typically include nine inner work steps that lead to forgiveness, emotional release, mind reset, increased peace, joy, and freedom in Christ:

1. Who to forgive and for what specifically;
2. What you made it mean;
3. Getting ready to release emotional residue;
4. Releasing, renouncing, and replacing that emotional residue;
5. Pronouncing forgiveness;
6. Identifying lies and other cognitive distortions and related unclean spirits;

7. Determining unholy ties, vows, unclean spirits, and curses;
8. Using the five keys from the gospel (listed below); and
9. Re-coding your mind with the truth.

If this process of forgiving is new to you, you could begin by watching some of my podcasts, particularly Episode #15.

Good preparation usually leads to a good application of these steps. A great way to learn more about the process is to read at least Part One of Neil Lozano's book, *Unbound: A Practical Guide to Deliverance*, and take notes. It's full of illustrative stories that may remind you of situations and events in your own life. The book explains how the Gospel's five keys can open you to the abundant life Jesus promised and close the entryways by which evil spirits gain access to your life.

The five keys are: repentance and faith; forgiveness; renouncing the work of your enemies; standing in the authority you have in Christ; and receiving God's blessing on your identity and destiny.[31] I believe the *Unbound* book can be a game-changer for every Christian. It's incredibly effective in teaching awareness and renunciation of unclean spirits.

The emotional release work and the re-coding of your mind I describe are not part of the Unbound prayer method Neal Lozano and Heart of the Father Ministries® teach. However, after using the Unbound prayer model, I find that a separate session for emotional release and re-coding of the mind adds another layer of healing, all of which can only happen with forgiveness. Most importantly, remember there are remedies and the power to overcome in the Holy Name of Jesus.

Other issues commonly addressed in Healing and Deliverance or Inner Work include identifying and, hopefully, putting an end to unhealthy habits (the sinful nature, discussed earlier), addictions, and

---

[31] Neal Lozano, *UNBOUND: A Practical Guide to Deliverance*, 2003, 2010, Chosen Books (Baker Publishing Group, Grand Rapids, MI, page 57.

habitual sins and idols, as well as occult influences.[32] Other issues in inner work and healing include unholy physical and spiritual soul ties, generational curses, what is generally called "stinking thinking," and what we call "gunk, funk, and junk" among my transformational coaching peers. The issues in quotation marks are professionally described as negative or irrational thoughts that lack evidence yet influence how you feel and behave. It's extremely beneficial to replace such distortions with life-giving qualities and the truth, through a process I call re-coding the brain to enable joy.

Identity Issues

Sadly, most of God's children are caught in an identity crisis, just as I was in my spiritual immaturity (*cf.* Ephesians 4:13-14). Not that I don't still fall into forgetful complacency about who I am in Christ; I sometimes do. At times, we must employ effective

---

[32] If you have dabbled in the occult, or if your family members were involved in it, occult influences need to be cast out even if the only dabbling was seemingly insignificant (such as reading horoscopes or playing with a Ouija board). That's because those activities and more intense occult involvement can be entryways for seeking knowledge from an ungodly source. Demonic influence can come to a person in relationships with other people affected by it and it can be quite oppressive, but it can be broken!

spiritual practices to break out of lies, unhealthy habits, and other hindrances in order to live as one's true self—obstructions such as fear, self-pity, false notions of identity and limitations, pride and false humility, and especially, an independent spirit that ignores the fact that on our own, we are nothing; but in Him, all things are possible, and we are His blessed daughters and new creations. (See John 8:28, Mark 14:36, Galatians 6:15).

Because of who your Father and Brother are, no weapon formed against you will prevail (Isaiah 54:17). Believers are authorized to use the name of Jesus in to drive out whatever's unclean or a spiritual hindrance (2 Thessalonians 3:6, Proverbs 23:7 KJV). As disciples, we're encouraged to make requests of our Father in Jesus' name, expecting Him to grant what we ask in faith (John 15:16). God made great promises we can count on.

I know I've repeated this often, as I do when talking to myself, sometimes numerous times a day. The promise is that the Father will work all things together for our good, whatever the circumstances, however challenging the situations are, even persecution and suffering (Romans 8:28, see 2 Timothy 3:11).

God is Love, Creator, Sovereign, Mighty, and more (*see* 1 John 4:8, Isaiah 40:28, Daniel 5:21, Zephaniah 3:17). Remind yourself that you are His masterpiece, awesomely and wonderfully made, thoroughly equipped for your mission. You're a beloved daughter of the Most High, chosen and set apart as a royal priesthood, called into God's marvelous light.[33] You were created in His image and likeness.[34] He provides you with a decisive guidebook known as The Holy Bible. Spend time with it. Take advantage of this free "life coach" offer: God is available for free, private consultations 24/7/365.

If your self-image is distorted from how God sees you, it's time for inner work to replace who you think you are with who God says you are. Your actions, feelings, behaviors, and abilities flow from your own beliefs. It's so important not to identify with your failures, sins, or old messages you've retained since childhood.

---

[33] See Ephesians 1:3, 2:10 NLT, Psalm 139:14 NASB, 2 Timothy 3:17, Psalm 82:6 NLT, 1 Peter 2:9 ESV.
[34] See Genesis 1:27.

The second half of life is an ideal time to engage in this process and reap the rewards of more expansive emotions and greater fruitfulness, using your God-given gifts, skills, talents, and abilities as a good steward. Express yourself fully, being kind and loving but not necessarily society's version of "nice." Then watch what unfolds, like the desires of your heart, creativity, and joy.[35]

If our goal is to think like Jesus, live in joy and alignment with God's will, and walk in the Spirit, loving as Christ has loved us and loving God with all our minds, hearts, and strength, guess what else? We must stop complaining, judging, and relying upon ourselves as if we are gods. C.S. Lewis spoke with profound faith about reliance on God to direct us in every decision every day.[36] He spoke of

---

[35] Maxwell Maltz, MD, FICS, Psycho-Cybernetics, updated and expanded, 2015, Tarcherperigee, an imprint of Penguin Random House LLC, Chapter One, "The Self-Image: Your Key to a Better Life," pages 1-15.

[36] Sarah Pangburn, "As If Nothing Had Yet Been Done," RelevantChurch.cc, The Gathering 2017 Summer Devotional Series, https://relevantchurch.cc/as-if-nothing-had-yet-been-done/, accessed October 9, 2024. (In my opinion, this article and its C.S. Lewis quotes are amazingly provocative and well worth pondering, and her article has influenced this part of my writing.)

happiness and joy being impossible unless we are walking with God.[37]

The Eternal Father's identity is "Our Father in heaven" (Matthew 6:9). He is holy, and we are to praise Him (*id.*) The crux of His plan is for His will to be done on earth as it is in heaven—that is, for us to change our lives because, through Jesus, God's Kingdom (the Kingdom of Heaven) is already here (Matthew 3:2, NIV and *The Message*). In other words, the Creator wants to extend His Kingdom throughout the earth to fully enforce Jesus' victory over the adversary.

On the other hand, the primary purpose of our spiritual opposition is to destroy us and derail us not only from joy but from God's path. That's why we ask in the prayer Jesus taught us to be delivered from evil.

---

[37] 27 Christian Quotes from C.S. Lewis, Great American Pure Flix INSIDER, https://www.pureflix.com/insider/27-christian-quotes-from-c.s.-lewis-youll-love, accessed October 9, 2024. The full quote is: "God cannot give us a happiness and peace apart from Himself, because it is not there. There is no such thing."

PRAYER

Jesus, would You please grant that I may know, love, and serve You with strong faith so I can recognize Your voice and the Father's will? Please, Lord, pour out Your grace to help me yield to You and make You the Master of the free will You've given me. Please free me from the impediments to faith, love, and joy!

Holy Spirit, would You empower me to transform my limiting beliefs into the truth that sets me free? Would You please reveal Jesus to me more clearly and intimately than ever before, drawing me close and never letting me go? Would You please show me how to walk with You, talk with You, and listen to You? Please help me see who I was created to be. Thank You, loving Abba Father, Jesus, and Holy Spirit

REFLECTION QUESTIONS
(For Individual Use or with a Small Group)

1. How much are you motivated in your daily choices by thoughts of Eternal Life, and why do you think that is?

2. With 24 New Testament verses instructing us to rejoice, what would it take for you to actively, and consciously respond with delight all the time? What things do you normally think about that you would have to give up?

3. Can you relate to Full Expression Avoided and Resisted? Did you grow up hearing things such as those listed in the F.E.A.R. section, and can you add others that contributed to limiting beliefs or a poor self-image? Will you aim to express your voice, uniqueness, and gifts more than you currently do?

4. Reflect on which aspects of Spiritual Poise would be most helpful to you: graciousness, confidence, humility, elegance, faithfulness, remaining relaxed and unflustered, compassion, and being responsive rather than reacting?

5. Have you done or would you be open to doing any intentional "Inner Work" for emotional release, replacing limiting beliefs with truth, and/or mental re-coding to free you and transform your mindset to think more like Jesus? What needs to be released, replaced with the truth, or transformed?

Chapter 5
Who is the Holy Spirit and What Does Life in the Spirit Look Like?

The sending of the promised Holy Spirit was a great source of joy. Saint Paul's prayer in Romans 15:4 is, "May the God of hope fill you with all joy and peace in believing, so that by the power of the Holy Spirit you may abound in hope." No wonder joy is strengthening, uplifting, and fruitful. Notice, God fills you with joy, peace, and hope, which become abundant through none other than the Holy Spirit!

We Need to Be Filled with the Holy Spirit...

In Chapter One you read my Baptism in the Holy Spirit story and my assertion that I've been on fire for God through the Holy Spirit ever since that event in 1989.

You might be lukewarm if you haven't yet been set on fire for the Lord. The Book of Revelation bluntly tells us that Jesus would like to spit out those who are lukewarm, so let's pray for your baptism in the Holy Spirit, which can set you on fire, figuratively, of course. We also *need* the Holy Spirit's power.

...For Miracles and Supernatural Stories

The Spirit can impact our lives in ways similar to what occurred in Biblical times. The Holy Spirit was active in the lives of Zachariah and Elizabeth, John the Baptist, Jesus, Mary, Simeon, Anna, and the disciples after Pentecost. The common element in those Spirit-filled figures was experiencing miracles and supernatural knowledge or power.

...To Build Up the Kingdom of God

In the Book of Acts, there are many instances of people being baptized or "filled" with the Holy Spirit and then used to help build God's Kingdom. Look at these examples scattered throughout the New Testament:

- In Acts 8:15-17, after hearing that Samaria had accepted the word of God, the apostles in Jerusalem sent Peter and John to Samaria. "When they arrived, they prayed for the new believers there that they might receive the Holy Spirit because the Holy Spirit had not yet come on them; they had simply been baptized in the name of the Lord Jesus. Then Peter and John placed their hands on them, and they received the Holy Spirit."

- In Acts 9:17-20, we see that the Lord sent a Damascus disciple named Ananias to place his hands on Saul. Ananias did that, saying, "Brother Saul, the Lord—Jesus, who appeared to you on the road as you were coming here—has sent me so that you may see again and be filled with the Holy Spirit." As soon as he placed his hands on him, something like scales fell from Saul's eyes. He had been blinded by his encounter with Jesus on the road to Damascus, and after this, he could see again. He was baptized and soon renamed Paul, and he began preaching Jesus in the synagogues.

- In Acts 10:44-45, the circumcised believers with Peter were astonished that the Holy Spirit had been poured out on Gentiles; in fact, the Holy Spirit came on all who heard Peter's message.

- In Acts 11:15-17, Peter reported to the church about the Spirit falling upon people in Joppa as he was speaking to them in the same way the Spirit had come upon the apostles, and he remembered what Jesus had said, that John baptized with water, but they'd be baptized with the Holy Spirit; and who was he to think he could stand in God's way of that happening?

- In Acts 19:1-6, Paul asked twelve disciples in Ephesus if they received the Holy Spirit when they first believed. They hadn't even heard that there is a Holy Spirit; they'd only received the "baptism of repentance" and belief in Jesus. Then, "when Paul placed his hands on them, the Holy Spirit came on them, and they spoke in tongues and prophesied."

- Galatians 3:14 says, "[Christ] redeemed us so that the blessing given to Abraham might come to the Gentiles through Christ Jesus so that by faith we might receive the promise of the Spirit."

- 2 Peter 1:21 says that prophecies can only be brought forth by the Holy Spirit.

- In 1 Thessalonians 1:6, we learn that we are chosen by God when, by the grace of the Holy Spirit, we receive the gospel not simply as words but also with power and deep conviction.

...To Strengthen Us to Resist Temptation and Walk More Uprightly.

All those scriptures illustrate that the Holy Spirit is essential, even if some people in mainline religions have overlooked, misunderstood, or downplayed this third person of the Trinity. We truly need the Spirit. For the Spirit is willing, but the flesh is weak (Matthew 26:41, Mark 14:8). Because the flesh (our human nature) is weak, we need help from the Holy Spirit, which the Father and Jesus willingly send to us and urge us to embrace. Through Jesus' saving blood and the power of the Holy Spirit, we can better resist worldly temptations, desires, and "stinking thinking," and walk by the Spirit into the uplifted position of children of God. All of those are impediments to joy, therefore this benefit of the Spirit keeps the door open for joy.

...And to Grow in Intimacy with the Holy Trinity

Through the Spirit, we're able to put God first in our hearts and minds—not 100% of the time because we are still human beings. Like Saint Paul and many holy men and women before us, we are meant to dedicate ourselves to knowing, loving, and serving God to the best of our intentions and abilities, so help us, God! This devoted lifestyle isn't easy, but we are also fully known by our God, who is gracious, merciful, compassionate, and understanding. He desires an intimate relationship with each of us, His beloved. Knowing the other and being known is central to developing a joyful love relationship, in this case with God.

Keys to a Profound Prayer Life

This section is about baptism by water and baptism in the Holy Spirit. I include it in a book about joy because my baptism in the Holy Spirit was the height of joy for me and a source of ongoing exuberance for God and for life. If you've already experienced this, you know exactly what I mean. I was in Rome for the 50th anniversary of the Catholic Charismatic Renewal, a gathering of 20,000 people baptized in the Holy Spirit, and I've never seen such effusive joy. Strangers were dancing and singing together to praise the Lord, and the experience of unity in the Body of Christ was extraordinary.

To Enter the Kingdom, You Must Be Born of Water and the Spirit

The first sign through which Jesus revealed His glory and His disciples began to believe in Him was at the wedding in Cana, when He turned water into wine (John 2:11). After that, the Gospel of John mentions they spent a few days in Capernaum, and just before Passover, Jesus went to Jerusalem and overturned the tables of the moneychangers in the temple courts, expressing zeal for His Father's house (John 2:13-17). While at the Passover Festival, some people saw the signs He performed and believed in Him (John 2:23).

Nicodemus came to Jesus secretly, because he was a Pharisee who knew, based on the signs Jesus performed, that Jesus came from God. Jesus told Nicodemus, "No one can see the kingdom of God unless they are born again" (John 3:1-3). Nicodemus asked for a further explanation of how an older person could be born a second time, and Jesus replied:

> "Very truly I tell you, no one can enter the kingdom of God unless they are born of water and the Spirit. Flesh gives birth to flesh, but the Spirit gives birth to spirit. You should not be surprised at my saying, 'You must be born again.' The wind blows wherever it pleases. You hear its sound, but you cannot tell where it comes from or where it is going. So it is with everyone born of the Spirit."

John the Baptist prepared the way for Jesus, preaching, teaching repentance, and baptizing, but John said:

> "I baptize you with water for repentance, but he who is coming after me is mightier than I, whose sandals I am not worthy to carry. *He will baptize you with the Holy Spirit and fire.*" ~ Matthew 3:11 ESV (emphasis added)

Though John tried to talk Jesus out of being baptized, Jesus insisted on being baptized "for we must carry out all that God requires" (Matthew 3:15 NLT).

There Are Two Kinds of Baptism

"After his baptism, as Jesus came up out of the water, the heavens opened and he saw the Spirit of God descending like a dove and settling on him. And a voice from heaven said, 'This is my dearly loved Son, who brings me great joy' (Matthew 3:16-17 NLT). That baptism in water marked the beginning of His public ministry. His disciples were also baptized in water, and when they went about evangelizing, Jesus instructed them to baptize in the name of the Father, Son, and Holy Spirit. These verses together certainly support that there are different kinds of baptisms. At that time, the disciples had not yet experienced their own infilling with all the power and charisms of the Holy Spirit, which came on Pentecost.

Baptism for the Forgiveness of Sins Imparts Graces and Membership

The Holy Spirit comes to us in water Baptism and imparts a grace that forgives all sins, makes us new creations as adopted children of the Father and co-heirs with Jesus, and temples of the Holy Spirit.[38] The baptized become members of the Church, uniting all the baptized into one Body of Christ (Ephesians 4:25, 1 Corinthians 12:13).

Through His promises of Baptism, God enables us to share His divine nature and escape the world's corruption caused by human desires (2 Peter 1:4 NLT). The baptized share in Christ's priesthood and His prophetic and royal mission (1 Peter 2:5, 9). The baptized no longer belong to themselves but to Jesus; therefore, they are expected to profess their faith and share the Good News (*cf.* 1 Corinthians 6:19, 2 Corinthians 5:15).

Baptism in the Holy Spirit Imparts Power and Often Ignites Dormant Gifts

Being baptized in the Holy Spirit is a Pentecost-like experience that empowers disciples far beyond what comes with water baptism for the forgiveness of sins. Therefore, Jesus told His disciples that it would be better for them if He went to the Father

---

[38] Catechism of the Catholic Church, Ascension Edition, 2022 ("CCC"), ¶1263, ¶1265 citing 2 Corinthians 5:17, *cf.* Galatians 4:56, 2 Corinthian 6:15; 12:27, Romans 8:17, 1 Corinthians 6:19.

because then He and the Father would send them an advocate, the Holy Spirit, the Spirit of Truth. Assuring His disciples about the Holy Spirit's power that is released through a Pentecost experience or anointing, Jesus said:

> *"For John baptized with water, but in a few days you will be baptized with the Holy Spirit."* ~Acts 1:5 (emphasis added)

Baptism in the Holy Spirit Can Occur Before, During, or After One's Water Baptism

In my experience, and it seems for most, baptism in the Holy Spirit comes after a water baptism. This order is supported by Acts 8:16, which says of the Samaritans who had accepted God's message, "the Holy Spirit had not yet come on any of them; they had simply been baptized in the name of the Lord Jesus." This is also the case in Acts 11:16, "Then I remembered what the Lord had said: 'John baptized with water, but you will be baptized with the Holy Spirit.'"

Like many Catholics and people in other sacramental denominations, I was baptized in water as an infant. It wasn't until I was forty that I was baptized in the Holy Spirit. I hadn't asked for or expected that baptism. As described in Chapter One, I was baptized in the Holy Spirit after deep repentance and confession of my sins, right in the confessional. In Acts 2:38, I found scriptural support for what I experienced—baptism in the Holy Spirit occurring with repentance.

To those who heard his sermon at Pentecost and asked what they should do next, Peter replied, "Repent and be baptized, every one of you, in the name of Jesus Christ for the forgiveness of your sins. And you will receive the gift of the Holy Spirit." Peter expected their baptism would combine the traditional baptism of repentance with receiving gifts of the Holy Spirit, but that doesn't always happen. It didn't happen to Jesus' apostles, and it didn't occur to the Samaritans.

In my thirties, I was in a close circle of four moms who had firstborn daughters born within a few weeks of each other. None of us were active followers of Jesus at the time. Two of us had been raised Catholic, but weren't practicing the faith. One's parents brought her up in a Protestant denomination, and the other was Jewish. We started to explore spirituality. The other "lapsed Catholic" experienced a miracle that enlivened her faith again and induced her witness to the rest of us, which led me to confession and my conversion.

One day, the Jewish woman was at the beach when she picked up a piece of green sea glass that led her into a profoundly sublime experience. When a ray of sunlight passed through the sea glass, the Creator took her on a journey so beautiful and miraculous that I don't want my words to do it injustice.[39] Not even a Christian, she was baptized in the Holy Spirit on the beach that day.

This is an example of what's described in Acts 10:47: "Surely no one can stand in the way of their being baptized with water. They have received the Holy Spirit just as we have." Soon afterward, she was baptized with her children, and not long afterward, she became a Catholic.

---

[39] See Bette Helaine Singer Harrison, *What Is a Nice Jewish Girl Like* me *Doing in Doing in the Catholic Church? 2018*, Chapter 13.

The Heart of a Joyful Spiritual Life is Encountering Jesus, which the Holy Spirit Can Bring About.

The Holy Spirit leads us to encounter and know Jesus. To be like Jesus, we must be able to love— acting, praying, or hoping for the good of others— no matter what. On my Hallow Catholic prayer and meditation app (see hallow.com), I enjoy episodes of the *Daily Holy Spirit with Father Dave*, recorded by Father Dave Pivonka, TOR, the President of Franciscan University of Steubenville and a vibrant and well-known speaker and author. Though he may have spoken chiefly to Catholics, Father Dave reports that when he asks people what they must do to get to heaven, few mention the importance of having a personal relationship with Jesus.

In a *Daily Holy Spirit* episode called "Encountering Jesus," Father Dave said that the heart of the spiritual life is encountering Jesus. We should pray for the Holy Spirit to lead us to this if we haven't yet had such an encounter. We have nothing without Jesus, he says.

Pope Benedict XVI said at a conference of bishops: "Being a Christian is not the result of an ethical choice or a lofty idea but an encounter with an event, the person, an encounter with Jesus, which gives life a new horizon and a decisive direction, thanks only to this encounter or renewed encounter with the love of God."[40]

It's not enough to just know about Jesus and some Bible stories. Being able to pass an exam on Jesus isn't enough. Look at the story of the Samaritan woman at the well in John's Gospel, chapter four. She encounters someone (none other than Jesus) who sees, accepts, challenges her, and loves her differently. She'd gone to fetch water in the noonday sun to avoid the townspeople.

After the encounter, she leaves her water jar behind and dashes off to tell everyone in her village that Jesus could be the Messiah. She told everyone, the very people she used to avoid because of her tainted reputation, and they came streaming from the village to see Him. She becomes an evangelist (John 4:1-42 NLT), not even trying to hide that Jesus told her everything she ever did. This is the kind of encounter where Jesus becomes the center of your life, by which your joy can be complete.

---

[40]Pope Benedict XVI, "Deus caritas est" (God is Love encyclical), 2005. *See References at the back of the book.

Sadly, not all regular churchgoers have a personal relationship with the Father, Son, or Holy Spirit. I was an example. Growing up, I heard the weekly readings (the rest of the Mass was in Latin), went to religious education classes, prayed at home before meals and at bedtime, and had some understanding of who Jesus was and what the basic teachings of Christianity were. That wasn't enough to keep me faithful through college and early adulthood.

Jesus and the Holy Spirit Set Us Free

Though co-equal with God the Father and Jesus the Son, the Holy Spirit is often passed over or ignored—a big mistake! "Where the Spirit of the Lord is, there is freedom" (2 Corinthians 3:17). Not only is the Holy Spirit the sanctifier, but it's also the Spirit who shows us Jesus, which is why a personal relationship with the Holy Spirit is a crucial, essential, and primary aspect of Christian life. Billy Graham said, "Many people have come to Christ as the result of my participation in presenting the Gospel to them. It's ALL the work of the Holy Spirit."[41] That's why in John 16:7, Jesus told us it was

---

[41] See *Unbound Ministry Guidebook: Helping Others Find Freedom in Christ* (2011, 2014) by Neal Lozano and Matthew Lozano.)

better for us that He was going away because that was a prerequisite for our Advocate, the Holy Spirit, coming to us!

So, if you haven't felt the tangible Presence of the Holy Spirit in your life, I urge you to pray for it! Look for a *Life in the Spirit Seminar*, which is a series of talks widely offered to help individuals pray for the Holy Spirit to come into their lives in a fuller way.[42]

Close Relationships with the Trinity Lead to Joy

A relationship based on a spiritual encounter with Jesus is likely to facilitate four key components of a fulfilling (and therefore joyful) spiritual life:

- the ability to set the priorities the Lord wants you to have;
- operating out of a Godly mindset;
- being faith-filled; and
- a rich prayer life and spiritual gifts to build up others in their faith.

---

[42] See, e.g., Office of Catholic Charismatic Renewal Services, Diocese of Rockford, Illinois, "What is a Life-In-the-Spirit Seminar," *See References at the back of the book.

How do these play out?

God proved His love for us while we were still sinners, and the blood of Christ saved us from God's wrath or condemnation, reconciling us to God (Romans 5:8-10 NASB). Accordingly, we can now rejoice in our wonderful new relationship with God. Jesus' sacrifice has made us amazing friends of God (Romans 5:11 *The Message*).

Remaining distanced and impersonal or not being moved to love God is not the kind of relationship the Lord wants. The Father has an immense heart for His children. Jesus' name, Emmanuel, means God with us. He wants to abide in us and us in Him. With this kind of intimacy is the benefit of no longer being His servants but rather His friends (*cf.* John 15:15).

Friends spend time together, converse, and enjoy one another's company. Friends don't ignore what the other asks of them or participate in what the friend invites them to do together merely out of a sense of duty but more likely out of love, camaraderie, cooperation, or affection. The friendship brings them joy.

Joy in Communal Prayer and Worship

Praying and worshiping in community also brings many people joy, like my experience in Rome and with a smaller group on pilgrimages, especially to the Holy Land. Communal prayer may include the Sabbath, holy days, holiday worship, and especially for Catholics (but all are welcome), even daily Mass, often combined with group prayers such as the Rosary or contemplative Eucharistic Adoration.

While communal prayer and worship differs from solo quiet times of listening for the voice of God, the Lord often speaks to our spiritual ears or hearts through the liturgy's words, the Bible readings, preaching, the lyrics of the music, or in the sacred silence.

You may want to always bring something handy for taking notes (especially if your second-half memory bank has a lot of its storage capacity full already). Taizé prayer services, charismatic prayer groups, and intercessory prayer groups are often on a recurring schedule. When people feel like praising God, especially in community, they frequently express their exuberance for God, life, and blessings in shouts of joy (see Psalm 33:3, 35:27). Much prayer is also sung, which many think is doubly effective.

When praying with a group, particularly a group that includes people baptized in the Holy Spirit, the charismatic gifts of the Spirit described in 1 Corinthians 12 are often shared. These include inspired spiritual gifts of wisdom, words of knowledge, supernatural faith, gifts of healing by the Spirit, mighty deeds (miracles), prophecy, discernment of spirits, tongues, and interpretation of tongues, all produced by the Holy Spirit (1 Corinthians 12:8-11). It's important to remember that "to each individual the manifestation of the Spirit is given for some benefit" (1 Corinthians 12:7), so Christians should "strive eagerly for the greatest spiritual gifts" to benefit the Body of Christ (*id.* at 31).

You also may hear a word of encouragement or a prophetic or healing word from another person in attendance. Stay attuned. I always leave the twice-a-week charismatic prayer meetings I attend (on Zoom) with at least one nugget of wisdom, encouragement, conviction, or exhortation. Contact me if you have never attended such a meeting and feel called to experience one. A Friday meeting is open to Catholics and other Christians genuinely interested in a Holy Spirit-centered prayer meeting.

As the prophet Joel foretold (Joel 2:28-32) and Peter declared on Pentecost, "'In the last days, God says, I will pour out my Spirit on all people. Your sons and daughters will prophesy, your young men will see visions, your old men will dream dreams. Even on my servants, both men and women, I will pour out my Spirit in those days, and they will prophesy'" (Acts 2:17-18). In contemporary prayer groups, some of the faithful also receive visions, and the Holy Spirit may lead others to share their interpretations with the other participants. Watching the Spirit actively at work in this kind of prayer meeting is beautiful and joy-filled.

What is Walking By the Spirit and Why Does It Matter?

Walking by the Spirit is also translated as letting the Holy Spirit guide your life, and then you will not gratify what your sinful nature craves (Galatians 5:16 NLT). The sinful desires are in opposition to the Spirit and keep people from inheriting the Kingdom of God. The list includes having anyone or anything as an idol, rivalry, jealousy, furious outbursts, selfishness, envy, and drinking bouts, in addition to the more obvious immorality and impurity (Galatians 5:17-21 NLT).

Walking by the Spirit fortifies your self-control. The same chapter says when you live by the Spirit, you've placed your faith in Christ (Galatians 5:5-6 NLT). When you walk by the Spirit, your identity and self-image typically go up in terms of understanding how beloved you are, whose you are, and that you have a sacred calling you were created and equipped for. Faith is expressing itself in love (Galatians 5:6 NLT).

You enjoy God's blessings, favor, and provision now, as well as an everlasting inheritance. If you are set free in Christ, you have the holy boldness to speak the truth in love, to express your thoughts, needs, and wants, and to witness to the Lord. You live that way (Jesus' Way, Truth, and Life) without fear of rejection, comparison, judging, condemnation, or loss of something you can't do without. You no longer have to fake it; you are the REAL you. You love God, others, and yourself, and you are Joy-Full!

This ideal—the REAL you—no longer believes limiting lies. All is forgiven—no more grudges, taking offense, or offending or hurting others. You understand what God asks of you, and you communicate with the Father, Son, and Holy Spirit all the time. You live by the Word of God and comprehend spiritual principles. In God, you live, move, and have your being (Acts 17:28).

Abiding in Christ, with Christ abiding in you and in the Father, you are fruitful and ideally pruned. Jesus, the heavenly bread of life, nourishes you (John 6:35). Yoked to Jesus, docile through love rather than out of obligation, your work and burdens seem easy (Matthew 11:29).

Spiritual Poise is an Approach to Life that Must Be Intentionally Cultivated

Walking by the Spirit, you bear adversity with spiritual poise because, as explained in Chapter Four, you know Spiritual poise means knowing that circumstances are temporary. God is gracious and in charge, and any suffering because of your faith is an honor, showing you are like Jesus.

As you carry your cross, you help redeem the world. Because you have surrendered to the Lord, you joyfully trust God to guide and direct you, thus eliminating stress, doubt, confusion, and floundering. With His spiritual fruit, the Holy Spirit is the most excellent helper. (We will return to Spiritual Poise again in Chapter 6, for it is an antidote to various impediments to joy.)

OK, so that's the best version of our lives!

The Spirit Helps You Grasp Concepts Like Humility and Holiness

By the Holy Spirit, the Spirit of Truth, you also realize that you are absolutely nothing without God. Not only do you fall short of the glory of God; you are a sinner. You are not your sin, and God has removed your transgressions as far from you as the east is from the west (Psalm 103:12). But sin isn't gone from your life, is it? Pride? Judging? Criticizing? Negative or condemning self-talk? Willful resistance? Self-reliance? Self-pity? Disappointment? It's not easy to step away from all that every day.

You can't deserve or earn holiness. Making you holy is what Jesus did for you. He paid a huge price for you; you cost Him great suffering (1 Corinthians 6:20, 7:23). Jesus came and conquered sin and death, and He has made you a new creation (2 Corinthians 5:17, Galatians 6:15). But have you still given in to the ways of the world, to attachments, idols, and your own notions of love, justice, and especially, performance?

Though you fall short, God is always for you! God is the Victor. Yes, trials and tribulations and spiritual opposition exist. But you have God and His angels and the Hebrews 12 cloud of witnesses on your side. You have the Ephesians 6 armor of God to put on daily. You know to submit yourself to God, stand firm, resist spiritual opposition, and the devil must flee (Ephesians 6:14, James 4:7). Hallelujah! You also have the opportunity to grow spiritually through every affliction you face, whether that's an annoying customer service rep on the phone who doesn't help you at all or being diagnosed with cancer.

The bottom line is this: the Holy Spirit gives us gifts, fruit, and power! The Spirit:

- strengthens you and gives you incredible gifts: the spirit of the Lord, wisdom, understanding, counsel, might, knowledge, and reverential fear of the Lord (Isaiah 11:2);

- produces delightful fruit in you (love, joy, peace, patience, kindness, goodness, faithfulness, gentleness, and self-control (Galatians 5:22-23); and

- empowers you to witness, minister, and serve, with certain gifts to some and other gifts to others: the ability to give wise advice, special words of knowledge, a charism of supernatural faith, gifts of healing, miraculous powers, prophesy, discernment of spirits, and speaking or interpreting unknown languages (1 Corinthians 12:8-10).

Thank You, Holy Spirit! We do indeed need and want You in our daily lives!

PRAYER

Come and overshadow me, Holy Spirit, with peace, presence, and power. Let me know You are with me and in me today, Holy Spirit! Release in me Your gifts, fruit, and power, in Jesus' name, that I may join You and Your chosen ones to renew the face of the earth and help build up the Kingdom! Holy Spirit, please lead me to a transforming encounter with Christ, to know how He thinks and loves, so I can better imitate Him! Spirit of God, You dwell in me and are greater than the spirit of the world. Hallelujah!

REFLECTION QUESTIONS
(For Individual Use or with a Small Group)

1. What struck you as you read what Galatians 5 says about walking by the Spirit so you won't gratify your sinful cravings (including having anyone or anything as an idol (considered ahead of God when making choices), rivalry, jealousy, furious outbursts, selfishness, and drinking bouts, besides impurity and immorality?

2. All Scripture was inspired by the Holy Spirit and is meant for teaching (2 Timothy 3:16). This chapter was full of scripture about the Holy Spirit, including baptism in the Holy Spirit, charisms including word gifts, and extraordinary faith and miracles. How do you feel about how often contemporary churches (yours in particular) do or don't teach about the powerful role of the Holy Spirit?

3. The 1 Corinthians gifts include prophetic word gifts, healing and miracle gifts, and praying, singing, or speaking in tongues (often considered to be the Spirit praying through people in groans or utterings when

we don't know how to pray (see Acts 2:4 and Romans 8:23). Ask God to enlighten the eyes of your heart about Holy Spirit gifts and charisms. Write what you sense Him saying to you.

4. To what extent have you been filled with the Holy Spirit or had Pentecost-like experiences and become strengthened to resist temptation, become more intimate in your Holy Trinity relationship, received greater freedom, sanctification, or new spiritual gifts, fruit, or charisms? If not yet, do you want that? What will you do to invite a greater outpouring of the Holy Spirit into your life?

Chapter 6
What Are Some Prayers That Invite Two-Way Conversations With God?

While growing up and even through my college years, I thought of prayer as something I was supposed to do. Blessings before meals and kneeling for prayers at bedtime were de rigueur. Praying if I was scared was automatic, typically using rote prayers. Check off that box! After my Holy Spirit encounter, I knew immediately that a different kind of prayer was essential.

I had one particular friend who exhibited a gift of bold faith and spontaneous prayer. She's the first person I contacted after my Holy Spirit encounter. I began by listening at the intercessory prayer group she hosted. We'd start each week with spontaneous prayers: first for the Body of Christ, the world, then for the country, the state, our city and schools, our parish and its personnel, our families, and finally, for ourselves. Over time, I learned that prayer takes many forms and grows with practice. We don't start out just like people in the Bible who heard an audible voice like Moses on Mount Sinai (Exodus 31:18), those present at Jesus' baptism in the Jordan (Matthew 3:17), or Mary of Bethany at Jesus' feet in her home (Luke 10:39). But I also knew I wanted to keep growing more intimate with God through an evolving prayer life.

What Kinds of Prayers Can Change Your Life?

One of my first steps toward hearing God was to apply the lessons Linda Shubert taught through *The Miracle Hour: A Method of Prayer that Will Change Your Life*. This balanced and effective prayer approach by a Holy Spirit-filled woman has helped more than a million people in over 25 countries to pray. Prayer like this helped me start to turn off the negative voices in my head from my inner critic, old critical parent tapes accumulated over the years, voices from the evil adversary, and stinking thinking.

This booklet breaks an hour into twelve five-minute segments, providing an excellent list of ways to pray. At any time, you might choose to use any of them:

1. Praise
2. Singing to the Lord
3. Spiritual Warfare
4. Surrender
5. Release of the Holy Spirit
6. Repentance
7. Forgiveness
8. Scripture Reflections
9. Waiting for the Lord to Speak
10. Intercessions
11. Petitions
12. Thanksgiving

As a newbie, I used *The Miracle Hour* prayer sequence daily. Then one day I had an urgent need and dared to pray, "I'm sorry, God, I need Your help with a pressing decision, and I don't have a whole hour. Could You just tell me now, whether to do X or Y?" Guess what? He did! He also taught me that He wants to guide us in all things, all the time.

Now I can quiet myself for a moment or for hours, anytime, anywhere, and God is always present to guide, correct, instruct, protect, heal, or love me! We can have dry spells, but I find that if I show up in the quiet, believing God will be there, He will be.

Bible Roulette?

Another way to hear from God is to ask Him to lead you to a biblical passage He wants you to receive and apply to your life. Also soon after my conversion, I was asked to host a Christian Leadership Week coffee that Christian churches sponsored annually in Newport Beach and Irvine, California.

I lived in a small house and wasn't sure if it would accommodate all those who would come. I asked the Lord if I should say yes or no, and I heard yes and agreed. But between my "yes" and the actual event, a house foreseen in my dreams became available through a foreclosure sale. We looked at it and wanted that larger house, but it needed work before we could entertain there. Should I renege on my commitment or forgo the purchase?

I opened the Bible and, to my great surprise, with my eyes closed, my finger landed on 1 Peter 4:10 under the heading, "Hospitality." I read, "As each one has received a gift, use it to serve one another as good stewards of God's varied grace." I then knew the answer was "Neither! Buy the house." We did so, cleaned up the entry and living room, and furnished the downstairs with time to spare before hosting the coffee, which was well attended and touched hearts.

I have since been told that the "open and point" approach is based on a misguided expectation that leads some to play "Bible roulette," which is like forcing God to give you a message. At that early point in my walk with Jesus, however, I believe God knew my limitations and my desire for His guidance well enough to work that method for good. And since it advised me to do something that agreed with the Word of God, I was not misled.

Is Listening to God a Directive God's Given Us?

I imagine everyone would like to be able to hear God's voice regularly. Hearing how much He loves you and talking to Him about everything is a privilege of being in the family of God. But what kind of close relationship has only one person doing all the talking and never listening? The value of regular two-way conversations with the mastermind of the universe can't be understated.

The *"Shema,"* Deuteronomy 6:4, and the following verses in the Old Testament begin with the word, in English, "Hear:" "Hear, O Israel, the Lord our God is one Lord." Pious Jews consider this as one of the most important portions of Scripture: They write it on their phylacteries (prayer attire) and recite it at least twice a day.[43]

We *must* learn to hear from God. We are God's sheep, and He tells us, "If only you would listen to his voice today! ... Don't harden your hearts as Israel did" at times (Psalm 95:6-7 NLT). Jesus promised that we can hear His voice if we listen. He reaffirmed that He is the good shepherd, and His sheep hear His voice; He knows them, and they follow Him (John 10:27). Indeed, the assertion that His sheep hear His voice is a promise we can count on.

The miraculous voice from heaven at Jesus' baptism said, "This is my Son ... listen to him" (Matthew 17:5), and the same message came to Peter, James, and

---

[43] F. B. Meyer, Bible, Commentary, Dictionary, "Deuteronomy 6:1-19: HOW TO TREAT GOD'S WORDS," e-Sword X, Version 9.4 (40), © 2024, Rick Meyers.

John at the Transfiguration (Luke 9:35). Moses even foretold that God would raise up a great prophet (alluding to Jesus) and that the people "must listen carefully to everything he tells you," because anyone who will not or does not listen to Him will have dire consequences, being completely cut off from God's people (Acts 3:22-23).

You Can Learn How to Have a Two-Way Dialogue with God

For me, the teaching that hit the two-way dialogue prayer approach home was Dr. Mark Virkler's book (co-authored by his wife Patti Virkler), *4 Keys to Hearing God's Voice.*[44] That book and the related online teaching schooled me in a reliable way to hear God's *rhema* (his voice spoken to my spirit), including means of good counsel or confirmation. "The 4 Keys" to hearing God communicate are:

- Stillness (quieting yourself to be ready to receive);
- Vision (fixing your eyes on Jesus);

---

[44] Mark and Patti Virkler, *4 Keys to Hearing God's Voice*, Communion With God Ministries. *Continued in References at the back of the book. "

- Spontaneity (tuning into the Spirit's flow); and
- Journaling (writing).

Dr. Virkler learned the first two keys from Catholic priests Dennis Linn and Matthew Linn. He then combined them with the other two keys, which he discerned from Habakkuk 2:2-3. Interestingly, he later found a book from 1685 with very similar content, so a version of this approach is over 400 years old.[45]

"When you are quiet enough, and even when doing mindless activities, God speaks into your heart with spontaneous pictures, words, and thoughts and can guide and lead you personally through this type of meditation," Dr. Virkler says. He recommends journaling these two-way dialogues with God and ensuring they align with God's Word, confirmed through a trusted counselor, church teachings, or further discernment.

Of course, there are other ways to hear God's voice. Use whatever way works for you, but if you don't yet have your own effective listening practice, I believe

---

[45] Dr. Mark Virkler, "Would You Believe the 4 Keys Were Taught 400 Years Ago?" Communion With God blog, Dec. 20, 2022. *See References at the back of the book.

the *4 Keys* approach is supported by Scripture and tradition. I can attest that the *4 Keys* work and you can learn them online! Communion with God Ministries also offers a lovely thirty-minute "Walking with Jesus" meditation on their website.

Be Open to Rhema, But Test It

God desires His joy to be in you and your joy to be complete. But this outcome depends on your remaining in His love by heeding His word—the written Word (*logos* in Greek) and, also in Greek, the carefully discerned spoken word, *rhema*. (John 15:10,14, Matthew 4:4).

Dr. Virkler, the author of *4 Keys to Hearing God's Voice*, found sixty-six uses of the word *"rhema"* meaning "spoken word" in the New Testament (New American Standard Bible). Vine's Expository Dictionary notes that the significance of *rhema* is exemplified by Ephesians 6:17, which includes *rhema* in the armor of God. The passage lists one of the tools of spiritual warfare as "the sword of the Spirit, which is the *rhema* of God," referring not to the whole Bible but to the individual scripture the Spirit brings to our remembrance when we need it.[46] As we discuss hearing from God with our spiritual ears, it will be helpful to understand that *rhema* is not uncommon, but "spoken words" are not all oral and must be tested (2 Corinthians 13:1).

God May Communicate Through the Unexpected or Repetition

Another way of "hearing" from God is to pay attention to the unexpected. Being aware and alert to possible signs and wonders from God can help us learn what God wants us to know.

At a particularly tough time, when our high school daughter was pregnant, amazing things would happen to keep me peaceful. Here are a few examples:

- I had asked my Scripture Sisters to pray for our troubled teen whose eyes had been avoiding mine. The week before we learned about the pregnancy, one of the Bible study women gave me a very

---

[46] Dr. Mark Virkler, "All Uses of 'Rhema' in the New Testament," Communion With God Ministries, https://www.cwgministries.org/all-uses-rhema-bible, accessed October 10, 2024, *citing* Vine's Expository Dictionary notes.

prescient book, *Just Enough Light for the Step I'm On*,[47] which I read the first sleepless night after hearing that Ryan, then 16, was pregnant. My stomach was twisted in knots, and I didn't bother to go to bed because I knew sleep wouldn't come. The book convinced me to approach the situation one day at a time, not mentally sifting through the list of possible repercussions or other people's reactions.

- The comforting lyrics of song after song reassured me, such as: "I Rejoice in Your Love" by Gary Sadler,[48] and "Breathe" by Marie Barnett.[49] Yes, I told myself, I need to do both: rejoice in God's love and take deep breaths of gratitude.

- Only days after learning Ryan preferred to call the fetus "Hope" rather than "it," one of the Scripture readings at Mass was

[47] Stormie O'Martian, *Just Enough Light for the Step I'm On* (Eugene, OR: Harvest House Publishers, 1999).
[48] ©1994 Integrity's Hosanna! Music (Admin. by Capitol CMG Publishing (Integrity Music, David C Cook)
[49] ©1995 Mercy/Vineyard Publishing

Romans 5:5. The words of the verse include "Hope does not disappoint because of the love of God." As soon as we got home, I typed the full verse in a 24-point font and posted it on the bedroom door, where it remained as daily encouragement for all of us until the baby came home.

- I attended a Pastoral Council meeting where someone who didn't know about our situation brought an opening prayer that referred to the council members (of which I was one) as "midwives of hope." My tears welled up, hearing that confirming prayer!

- Ryan's water broke seven and a half weeks before the baby's due date, and ultrasounds showed his lungs were far from fully developed. The doctor hospitalized Ryan to help postpone the birth as long as necessary and arranged for my husband and me to visit the NICU to prepare us for the worst. Seeing all those teeny infants separated from their parents and hooked up to mechanical equipment, we wilted, anticipating what they were preparing us for. We enlisted our supporters to increase their prayers to bolster our family's prayers for a healthy mom and baby, and our Catholic friends offered many a rosary for these intentions.

- A month later, an ultrasound showed our grandson's lungs in good shape, so the medical team induced labor—on the Feast of Our Lady of the Rosary. Because our friends had been praying rosaries for our family since finding out about the pregnancy, inducing on that Marian feast day was such a welcome sign that I started dancing in the delivery room. Our grandson, born at 5 pounds, 5 ounces, was able to go home without spending time in the NICU, praise God! And isn't it fascinating that we had Romans 5:5 posted on the nursery door during his gestation and at birth he weighed "5-5?"

- Ryan named him Elliott, which means "The Lord is my God."

When a message or passage comes to you repeatedly over a day or a week, the unexpected repetition usually signals God trying to make a point crystal clear! For me, receiving a word or a message from God, a scripture that's just so on point, having an uplifting song pop onto the radio, or getting inspiration from a dream or a wise friend—all these also bring me great joy and reinforce how much God loves me!

How Does Sacred Scripture Help You Find Joy?

Jesus asks His followers to take His Word and His teachings seriously, to show the Way for others, so followers will find honor in the Kingdom of Heaven (Matthew 5:19 *The Message*). Knowledge of the Word of God is critically important, so incorporating into your life reading, studying, and praying with Scripture helps you align with God's will, which is part of the abiding, aligning vine and branches by which Jesus desires that our joy becomes complete.

Lectio Divina is Latin for "Sacred Reading," and it is a form of reading, meditating, and listening that is part of my daily prayer. (Though typically done with

Scripture, *Lectio Divina* also combines well with other inspirational writing, such as inspired poetry or daily reflections that are part of a novena or daily devotional.) I always journal what *Lectio Divina* reveals to me. The process rarely fails to help me receive from the Lord through the Holy Spirit.

The steps are:

1. <u>Reading</u>. Preferably read aloud or listen to a recording of a short Scripture passage, so you can hear the sacred Word and comprehend its "exegesis"—what the text says, what almost everyone would understand from its words as its intended meaning.

2. <u>Meditation</u>. After reading or listening to the passage again, slowly close your eyes and let the words sink in, noticing if particular words or aspects speak to you and your life. It might help to picture yourself in the passage's scene. This could bring up a memory or issue that you'll want to reflect upon or address.

3. <u>Prayer</u>. Next, talk to God in response to His Word. This personal encounter could involve asking, praising, thanking, seeking more understanding, or feeling God's presence and rejoicing.

4. <u>Contemplation</u>. Now contemplate how the passage or the Lord is bringing you some insight, inspiration, or understanding.

5. <u>Action</u>. As a result of encountering God's grace, discern what God's directing you to do—either about your special calling or other specific directions, especially if you believe you know your special calling.

My Lectio Divina and my *Walking with Jesus* mornings have brought me truly transformative encounters with the Holy Trinity. And those encounters help me radiate joy because I'm blessedly conversing with my Lord and Savior and the Holy Spirit daily (and some days with Abba Father)! I believe these prayer sessions can affect one's whole life, bringing "dead people to life." During one such meditation, Jesus affirmed me and encouraged me in a way He knew I needed to hear:

"Even now, you have that crown of gray hair and glory, and I applaud your desire to help others around your age (give or take decades). But it's not about what you do. You are loved, just being you. You DO out of love for 'Us3,' especially because you know the Holy Spirit well. I will increase your joy and your effectiveness. Enjoy everything you're doing. It will be part of your encounter with Me."

Note: I think of the Holy Trinity as three-in-one, and each person of the Trinity has a voice. In my journals, years ago, I began to address the Trinity as "U3" and, with God's sense of humor, I sometimes hear back from "Us3."

What Can You Learn About Joy from Immersing Yourself in The Bible?

Joy is widespread throughout the Holy Scriptures, even in the Old Testament, so reading, studying, and praying with the Bible will help you understand more of God and more about joy.

Humankind sinned, beginning with Adam and Eve, and moral evil entered the world. Yet God's providence can bring good even from the consequences of evil, as evidenced by the story of Joseph in Egypt speaking to his brothers in Genesis 50:20 (ESV): "It was not you who sent me here, but God ... You meant evil against me; but God meant it for good, to bring it about that many people should be kept alive."

Back then, the Lord also promised joy, which His people experienced in various instances. The Book of Psalms is known for expressing every human emotion and many qualities of mind and character. I'm fascinated that 82 of the 150 Psalms (55%) mention joy or rejoicing in the New International Version. Others express a glad attitude of the heart but use other terms or examples, such as Psalm 37:4, "Take delight in the LORD, and He will give you the desires of your heart." Psalm 35:27-28 (ESV) mentions joy, delight, and gladness:

> "Let those who *delight* in my righteousness shout for *joy* and be *glad* and say evermore, 'Great is the LORD, who *delights* in the welfare of his servant!' Then my tongue shall tell of

your righteousness and of your praise all the day long," said David (emphasis added).

Joy in God's Presence or Places Where His People Worship Him

In Leviticus 9:24, fire consumed a burnt offering on the altar and when the people saw it, they shouted for joy and fell facedown. In 1 Chronicles 29:22, there was joy in God's presence at the anointing of Solomon as king. First Chronicles 16:27 suggests that God intends for joy to abound in us.

In the New Testament, God's presence as joy is confirmed. In John 15:10-11, Jesus said those who keep His commandments will abide in His love so that His fullness of joy could be in us. Saint Paul clarified that we are not our own, for our bodies are temples of the Holy Spirit!

Since we are akin to God's dwelling place, where there is joy, I believe we are entitled to joy.[50]

---

[50] *Cf.* Psalm 42:4 and 43:4; Ezra 6:16 and 22.

Joy Upon Realizing God Is For His People

There's joy in knowing that God is *"for* us," demonstrated when the people of God in the Old Testament joyfully acknowledged: God's help and protection; healing (physical, emotional, or spiritual); guidance (directly or through wise counsel); unfailing love; statutes and precepts; trustworthiness; and salvation. They also spoke joyfully of the victories God helped them win, including delivering them from ungodly habits, addictions, temptation, and bondage, as well as for His awesome wonders, including ones that filled them with laughter.[51]

Note that this notion of joy coming from knowing that God is for us is also reconfirmed in the New Testament:

> "What, then, shall we say in response to these things?"—such as trouble, hardship, persecution, famine, nakedness, danger, or the sword—"If God is for us, who can be against us?" ~ Romans 8:31.

---

[51] Psalms 28:7; 30:11; 67:4; 90:14; 18:8, 119:111; 20:5; 65:8; 126:2; 94:19; 71:23, 105:43; 51:8, 95:1.

In Deuteronomy 16:15, the people experienced "complete" joy when celebrating God's blessing of their harvests and the work of their hands. In Psalm 81:1, they sang for joy in gratitude for their strength. King David rejoiced in the Lord's strength and expressed his great joy in the victories God gave him (Psalm 21:1).

So, shouldn't we be joyful when, with God's blessing, we bear good fruit, do good, or notice something so remarkable that we know it couldn't have occurred without God?

C.S. Lewis wrote in *The Great Divorce:*

> There are only two kinds of people in the end: those who say to God, "Thy will be done," and those to whom God says, in the end, "Thy will be done." All that are in Hell, choose it. Without that self-choice there could be no Hell. No soul that seriously and constantly desires joy will ever miss it. Those who seek find. To those who knock it is opened.[52]

---

[52] Ken Boa, Sunday Morning Study "Quotes from C.S. Lewis," Reflections with Ken Boa, *quoting* C.S. Lewis, *The Great Divorce*, chapter 9, https://kenboa.org/sunday-morning-study/quotes-from-c-s-lewis/, accessed October 10, 2024.

In Summary

The key to a powerful prayer life is a two-say conversation: talking to God, being still and knowing God (Psalm 46:10), which may include silence with your Creator Jesus, or the Holy Spirit. We may begin a time of prayer with gratitude and praise. We may present petitions for ourselves or intercede for others or for situations or conditions in the world. In this book, I've focused on the kinds of prayer I've found most helpful in encountering Jesus in a relational way, like silently hearing His voice.

If you'd like more ideas about prayer approaches, go to RadiantJoy.us/joy-book and I'll be delighted to send you a link to download a PDF on Fruitful Prayers as part of your gift package.

PRAYER

Jesus, thank You for Your hand and voice being outstretched to me. You delight in Your time with me even more than I do with You! Please satisfy my longing to experience Your divine presence, and send Your Holy Spirit to help me perceive Your communications to me and Your immense and abiding love. Great are You, Lord, and worthy of all praise. How wonderful that You want me to know You intimately by spending time alone with You. I might picture You, Jesus, lovingly holding me in a big embrace. May I receive with grace the visions and feelings, and treasure the words and sentiments You say to me in those precious times? Amen. Alleluia!

REFLECTION QUESTIONS
(For Individual Use or with a Small Group)

1. What kinds of prayer have changed your life? How has your prayer life varied from one season of life to another, if it has? Do you journal or use prayer apps?

2. The Good Shepherd says His sheep know His voice—probably not an audible voice! Scriptures mentioned in this chapter make hearing God's voice sound like a normal daily possibility. How's that working for you, and if it isn't, what will you practice?

3. What settings are most conducive to your best times of prayer: where, when, alone or with others, with what kinds of "things" (journal, pen, Bible, phone, tablet, coffee or tea, devotionals, prayer books, candles, flowers, prayer beads, etc.)?

4. Are there ways God communicates with you or gets your attention outside of your "dedicated prayer times," perhaps in unexpected ways, creativity, or nature? How would you describe what He does?

5. How do famous meditation, contemplation, adoration, and time with Scripture fit into your time with God?

Chapter 7
How Can Seasoned Women Embrace a Radiant Joy Lifestyle?

Live as a Good Steward

As described in the Introduction, each of us has been endowed by our Creator with every spiritual blessing under the heavens and every spiritual gift we need as we await Christ's final coming (Ephesians 1:31; Corinthians 1:7). Each of us is uniquely created for a particular mission to carry out with God's guidance and direction. He knows the desires in our hearts. He promises that when we delight in the Lord, He gives us our heart's desires (Psalm 37:4).

Our hearts plan our way, as Proverbs 16:9 tells us, but the Lord directs our steps. We are to seek the Lord's counsel and wisdom and ask Him to reveal what we need to know, do, embrace, or eliminate, clarifying the assignment, the steps, and the order He wants us to follow. We seek or ask, and when He tells or shows us the answers, we follow His plan and obey His directions faithfully. We don't need to know the How or the Outcome in advance, for those are up to Him. His ways are wiser than ours (Isaiah 55:9), so we'd be foolish to try to outsmart or outmaneuver God!

Having a goal in mind, and visualizing it already achieved, contributes to the desired outcome because imagining the completed result helps us to pray "believing, without doubt," or as worded in James, chapter 1, verses 6-8:

> "When you ask, you must believe and not doubt, because the one who doubts is like a wave of the sea, blown and tossed by the wind. That person should not expect to receive anything from the Lord. Such a person is double-minded and unstable in all they do."

Jesus' Parable of the Talents (Matthew 25:14- 30) illustrates the Kingdom of Heaven with a story of a man going on a journey and, while gone, entrusting his money (or talents) to three of his servants. The parable shows that the Lord, our Master, isn't unreasonable and doesn't overload us with unbearable tasks. We learn gradually, and He uses that to teach us about stewardship.

In the parable, two of those entrusted with the master's talents doubled the value, and the master (or "lord" in the King James Version) said, "'Well done, my good and faithful servant! Since you were faithful in small matters; I will give you great responsibilities. Come, share your master's joy'" (Matthew 25:21 NAB). In verse 29 (NLT), the master explains that to those who use what they are given well, even more will be provided to them, and they will have an abundance.

Not being a good steward of what the Lord entrusts to you has dire eternal consequences: the master calls the servant "worthless" who buried the talent out of fear and returned it just the same as when he received it. He throws that servant into the darkness with weeping and gnashing of teeth (Matthew 25:30).

Using your talents well during earlier parts of your life allows you to grow into greater talent or resources, which reinforces the idea that we may bear more good fruit for the Lord as we grow older and continue being His good and faithful stewards.

I know many older women who served in active, in-person ministries for years, learning and growing in their relationships with God along the way. Then, with less physical stamina in later years, or family concerns at home, they have moved away from church or one-on-one ministry into writing spiritual books, teaching online, and the like. They may reach more individuals now than before, for which their earlier in-person work prepared them.

As Saint Paul urges in Colossians 3:23-24, "Whatever you do, do it heartily, as to the Lord and not to men, knowing that from the Lord you will receive the reward," whether sooner or later.

We are sometimes put to a test of our faithfulness. The greatest example in scripture may be Abraham being called in Genesis 22 to sacrifice his son Isaac. Perhaps you have been asked to give up something you cherished. Are you willing to do what God asks, even if it seems senseless?

<u>A Story of Faith and Obedience Tested</u>

My charismatic prayer group leader, Kevin, gives a testimony about commissioning a priest he knew well to create an icon to adorn Kevin and his wife's home. When the priest, Father Damian, delivered the large icon, Kevin was overjoyed at its beauty. He would have paid whatever Father Damian asked. However, the priest had said each previous time he'd painted an icon for Kevin, "Pay whatever the Lord tells you to pay." So, before Father Damian arrived, Kevin prayed about how much to give him. When Father Damian delivered the icon, he said, "Whatever the Lord tells you to give me will be fine."

Kevin laughed and said, "I'm glad you said that because the Lord told me to pay you zero."

Father Damian's wide-eyed expression told Kevin his response surprised the priest, a talented and well-respected iconographer. But Father Damian simply said, "That's fine."

When Kevin tells this story, he says, "I admit I didn't feel good about it, but I know the Lord has had me do some bizarre stuff, and it always ends up glorifying Him."

Six months after delivering that icon, Father Damian visited Kevin and his wife and said, "I want to thank you for your obedience. When I painted your icon, I'd determined to use the money you would give me to help a Christian ministry that was just getting started in Sri Lanka. They had a little structure built on the beach and didn't have running water or other basics. When you told me you were giving me nothing for the icon, I was shocked and thought, 'Lord, these people have hardly anything, and now I can't help them.' I asked the Lord, 'Did Kevin hear You wrong, or was he being disobedient and just didn't want to part with the money?'"

He continued, "Four months after bringing you the icon, a tsunami hit that area and destroyed everything the ministry had built. Any money you would have given me would have gone to that ministry and would have been wasted." The December 26, 2004, Indian Ocean earthquake and tsunami, in which 230,000 people died, utterly wiped out the village where the ministry's school would have been constructed.[53]

---

[53] *See* Sevil Omer, World Vision, "2004 Indian Ocean earthquake and tsunami: Facts and FAQs," updated August 14, 2024, https://www.worldvision.org/disaster-relief-news-stories/2004-indian-ocean-earthquake-tsunami-facts, accessed October 9, 2024

After that conversation, the Lord led Kevin to give Father Damian a generous donation for painting the icon. The obedience brought them joy as they saw how the zero payment and timing accorded with what God knew rather than anything that Father Damian and Kevin would have reasoned or imagined on their own.

What is Inner Work, and What Difference Does It Make?

Many of us try to do too much, and we assume it's up to us to determine what to do and when. We can easily get wrapped up in busyness and stress. Okay, maybe you're no longer doing that, but you may be watching your adult kids get caught up in that way of living.

The pattern can lead to stress, impatience, insomnia, poor sleep habits, resentment, anger, and judging. If you are or used to be a perfectionist, an overachiever, or just overly committed or overwhelmed, consider this quote from Marie O'Connor: "It's not so much how busy you are, but *why* you are busy. The bee is praised. The mosquito is swatted."

Eighteen years ago, when I attended that Benedictine School for Charismatic Spiritual Directors, we were shown photos of a hundred animals and asked which one we most identified with. Not aware of the bee and mosquito analogy, and probably led by the Holy Spirit, I identified with an ant. I was unaware that ants can carry over 1,000 times their weight.[54] No wonder I ended up with surgery on both shoulders, my back, and my bladder, and broke both arms in one ice skating fall!

I had repeatedly failed to make the necessary changes in behavior or my thinking to yoke myself to Jesus and let Him do the heavy lifting.

We all need to challenge and overhaul old beliefs, on which we base our thoughts, choices, and actions, which affect our results. We may need to overhaul our self-concepts. Most of us need some high-level help to become You 2.0 because if this sort of inner work could be done thoroughly on our own, we'd

---

[54] Entomology Today, The Entomological Society of America, "Ants Can Withstand Pressure Up to 5,00 Times Their Own Body Weight," February 11, 2014, Research News, *citing Journal of Biomechanics,* https://entomologytoday.org/2014/02/11/ants-can-lift-up-to-5000-times-their-own-body-weight-new-study-suggests/, accessed October 6, 2024.

have done it already. We don't deal with some of our bondages because they're in our blind spots. This is why I'm a proponent of spiritual direction, spiritual cleansing, healing prayer, and transformational coaching provided by specially trained Christians. Most importantly, all of us need deep dialogue with God, and He is always available.

Thanks be to God, in recent years, I met with three transformational coaches and a spiritual director with amazing gifts of hearing God's voice and receiving wisdom, teaching, and miracles! From the Christian transformational coaches and from Dr. Mark Virkler of Communion with God Ministries, I've learned the importance of asking God questions to inform our beliefs, direct our choices, and transform our self-image and outcomes.

I hope and pray that I may help many of you along these lines through my writing, podcasting, workshops, Wisdom Circles, spiritual direction, and transformational coaching.

For example, Stephanie Richter (whose interview you can watch on Episode 19 of the Radiant Joy with Christine podcast) prompted me to ask the Lord and journal His responses to these questions:

- God, who are You?
- Would You please reveal Your loving and true nature to me?
- How do You see me, God?
- Who do You say that I am?
- What did You create me to do?[55]

(Those were only her identity questions; she has led me through many other check-ins with God on different topics—which I hope you'll get to read about in a book she's writing.) In a Holy Spirit-friendly environment, seeking God's input to a few questions like those may not take more than ninety minutes, and seeking His answers may redirect your whole life.

Every morning while writing this book, I asked God for encouragement and His solid counsel came forth every time I sat in stillness. You can have a meeting with God and ask for input on anything. Philippians 2:14 instructs us not to grumble or complain, but the exception is that you *can* pour out your heart to God, who welcomes that kind of honest communication (Psalm 142:2).

---

[55] *See* www.StephanieRichter.com.

You can ask Him what He wants you to know or what He wants you to do to resolve a problem, serve Him, or overcome a hindrance or habitual sin. You can ask financial, business, or relationship questions. God has the right answers for everything. Make dialoguing with Him a consistent practice. Your spiritual ears will improve at listening, and your joy will overflow.

You know the best antidote: Let go and let God! But let's rephrase that.

Let God tell you what to let go of! Ask Him, listen, and obey.

The Gardener knows what needs to be pruned. Don't be like a miserably sick patient who goes to a doctor and tells the doctor how to treat her before hearing the physician's recommendations.

Seek help and do inner work that focuses first on your identity and the self-image controlling your life.

Remember, you are endowed with every spiritual gift you need.

What we believe deep down is like the roots of the tree that represents the full-grown us. We must figure out what is hidden underneath the visible "tree." We need to identify and uproot false beliefs, lies, and all negative aspects of our self-image, replacing them with new beliefs—the truth that sets us free to be who the Creator intended.

These rotten roots (old, false beliefs) could be as severe and old as repeating what we picked up in childhood about not being good enough, never amounting to anything, being unworthy of love and attention, not belonging, being unsafe and unprotected, being used, abused, or falsely accused.

Hidden beliefs, which are really lies, might include: "I'm not good in big groups," or "I'm unable to learn new technology," or "I have no sense of direction," or—one of mine—"I'm time-zone challenged." So, in my case, guess what happens? All too often, I'll sign up for an online event and then miss it because I added three hours instead of subtracting three hours to convert from Eastern to Pacific time. Then I miss something I wanted to hear, reinforcing my belief that I truly am time-zone-challenged. Why don't I just use my calendar to enter the time zone for each event and let Apple or Google send me reminders based on the zone I'm currently in? Duh! Now I will do that!

Enjoy the Journey

In order to enjoy the journey before you and let your joy be full, Sacred Scripture gives us three key commands.

1. Trust and Obey God.

After Pentecost, the Sanhedrin brought the apostles before the high priest for questioning because they had defied strict orders not to teach in Jesus' name, yet they had done so and filled Jerusalem with their teaching. "Peter and the other apostles replied: 'We must obey God rather than human beings! The God of our ancestors raised Jesus from the dead—whom you killed by hanging him on a cross.'"

Members of the Sanhedrin became so furious they wanted to put the apostles to death, but a Pharisee and teacher of the law named Gamaliel, advised them to let the apostles go, saying, "For if their purpose or activity is of human origin, it will fail. But if it is from God, you will not be able to stop these men; you will only find yourselves fighting against God."

Gamaliel's speech persuaded them not to kill the apostles. They flogged them instead and ordered them again not to speak in Jesus' name, and then let them go. How did the apostles respond? With joy! They left the Sanhedrin "rejoicing because they had been counted worthy of suffering disgrace" for Jesus (Acts 5:27-41). Think about it!

2. Share the Good News.

Sharing our faith brings joy. When we evangelize or proselytize others and they come to Jesus, that brings us tremendous joy. As Saint Paul told the Thessalonians, "After all, what gives us hope and joy, and what will be our proud reward and crown as we stand before our Lord Jesus when he returns? It is you!" (1 Thessalonians 2:19 NLT). There is joy in sharing the Good News, even when it seems dangerous to do so.

On Easter morning, Mary Magdalene and several other women ran quickly from the tomb after being told by an angel that Jesus was not there and had risen (Luke 24:6). Matthew reports that they were very frightened, but also filled with great joy. And as they were heading away from the tomb, Jesus met them and greeted them. The women ran to Him, grasped His feet, and worshiped Him. Then Jesus sent them to bring the good news to the others, saying to them, "Don't be afraid! Go tell my brothers to leave for Galilee, and they will see me there" (Matthew 28:8-10 NLT).

3. Rejoice Always.

As discussed in Chapter 4, Saint Paul exhorted the Philippians and the Thessalonians to "Rejoice in the Lord always"—even in times of suffering or persecution, as Peter, Paul, Matthew, and Luke all wrote. Accordingly, let's live aligned with joy. Let's rejoice "and leap for joy" that our names are written in heaven, where we will see God (Luke 10:20; John 16:22).

We enter this world innocent, living in the present moment, expressing our needs and wants without holding back. We already have a divine identity, and

God already designed a plan for our lives. When Jesus says we need to become like little children to enter the Kingdom of Heaven (Matthew 18:3), I believe He encourages us to return to our Original Design and God's blueprint for our lives. And when we mess up or get off course, we can trust God to keep His promise to work it all out for good. Indeed, it may be in the most adverse circumstances that we:

- draw closer to God,
- develop the compassion or skills we need to carry out our Kingdom assignments,
- and learn how we need to be transformed...

...to live in a close personal relationship with God, aligned with our REAL self, and aglow with the love and light God wants to shine on the world through you and me.

Believing is key. Believing is trusting in God's answer or the manifestation you are certain will come (James 1:2-8). It also involves truly knowing who you are in Christ, who the Father, Jesus, and the Holy Spirit are. It means living with trust and joy, as well as a Sermon on the Mount heart (see Matthew 25) and a Saint Mother Teresa attitude. See Christ in everyone, love them, and imagine the infinite love and joy of the Great Creator!

In your quiet time, you might ask God more questions. God knows and wants to guide you to being your best self! Indeed, if you're thirsty for understanding, ask God, for Psalm 107:9 tells us "he satisfies the thirsty."

For example, I've asked Jesus about my long-held people-pleasing and approval-seeking tendencies. I learned that I was always trying to be "nice" (which is an ingrained cultural, sometimes inauthentic trait, different from being kind, caring, compassionate, and led by the Spirit).

After shedding light on that, the Holy Spirit strengthened me to bring my voice forward with honesty, integrity, and kindness, speak the truth in love, and ask for what I want or need. A step in that process involved asking God to reveal WHY I was such a people-pleaser. He revealed specific fears and beliefs underlying my false self-identity:

- Timidity about not being liked;

- A history of criticism about making even little mistakes, and a tendency to see them in others; and to make unhelpful comparisons; and

- Overthinking—fear of being wrong, judged, criticized, lazy, forgetful, or "too" something like white or Catholic, all of which leads to the imposter syndrome, self-editing, perfectionism, fear of inadequacy ("not good enough"), fear of not pleasing God, and fear of losing unbelieving loved ones.

At times, we all need to be corrected, to disagree, or to displease others. Even Jesus couldn't work miracles in Nazareth because of the unbelief! We are not made to people-please. I've tried that and it's exhausting and at times lacks integrity and alignment with God's will. Therefore, we need to accept that sometimes the most aligned and loving response will displease those who hear it. As for fear of not pleasing God, an insight came: the Father declared over Jesus that He was well pleased at Jesus' baptism before Jesus began His public ministry, according to Matthew!

Jesus didn't have to DO what He was on earth to do in order to please His Father.

The Father is pleased by our being ourselves and in relationship with Him, with the desire to know, love, and serve Him, especially (I think) in a surrendered state of love and trust, like a child who trusts her loving parent.

Most difficult and painful to the self is trying to be someone we're not, often based on messages and beliefs instilled from birth onward. As an active mom, I thought, "You have to bend over backward for your kids to like you." My mother made it seem that way, and I adopted the belief without realizing it. That underlying belief could make motherhood extra challenging! More importantly, with any false beliefs and negative attitudes, we end up heavily adapting, sometimes to survive, other times, striving.

If you do that, you may realize that it takes so much energy to keep up or to compensate for your perceived (but false) identity that you become tired, exhausted, and overwhelmed. Another possibility is that when you didn't feel seen and heard, you stopped trying to get the attention you wanted and settled for attachment.

The solution is to choose to BE YOURSELF! Love, Safety, Security, and Belonging are natural needs and desires. Inner work can help in all those areas. Seek the Spirit's guidance and ask for wisdom along with truth! Hopefully, you'll embrace truths such as these: God always loves me. I belong in God's family. I am fully loved as I am, not for what I do. You'll also be able to get directions for the next steps.

What About Grief and Trauma's Effects?

Jesus speaks of sorrow as temporary. If you've given birth, you may relate to His description of a mother following a difficult delivery, who afterward experiences great joy with her newborn (despite sleep deprivation). I had a long labor and then a Cesarean delivery with my first, and I initially thought I'd never want to give birth again. But joy from the gift of life changed my mind, and we were blessed with another child—thanks be to God—with a vaginal birth.

Jesus' disciples endured grief upon hearing Him foretell His leaving them and going to the Father. His reply is good for us to ponder in our times of sorrow as well:

> "So, you have sorrow now, but I will see you again, and your hearts will rejoice, and no one will take your joy from you. In that day you will ask nothing of me. Truly, truly, I say to you, if you ask anything of the Father, he will give it to you in my name. Until now you have asked nothing in my name; ask, and you will receive, that your joy may be full." ~John 16:23 ESV

Grief and trauma test our emotional, physical, and psychological capacity, often overwhelming our defenses. Trauma can result from the absence of good and necessary things we need all through our lives, often experienced as abandonment or loss, insecurity, and lack of caring.

Trauma also comes from bad things we don't know how to cope with, such as 9-11, devastating natural disasters such as tornados or hurricanes, mass shootings, abuse, or a raging parent. These conditions are joy killers when they exceed our capacity or emotional resilience to bounce back without buckling under the weight of grief or trauma. Conversely, joy builds one's capacity to bear adversity. Remember, the joy of the Lord is our strength (Nehemiah 8:10). And joy is a long-lasting state, not dependent on external circumstances.

Doing what you can now to increase your joy will then build your capacity to weather surprises that test your well-being. In the School of Healing Prayer patterned after Christian Healing Ministries, which I took at Hope in the Desert Episcopal Church ("SHP"), we were taught to stir joy in our souls in five ways:

- Practice gratitude because joy grows as you appreciate and thank God for all the ways He's blessed you;
- Reflect on times of joy with appreciation, remembrance, and sharing to keep the flames of joy burning and set the stage for more;
- Participate in a faith community where joy is shared and encouraged;
- Strip away what controls you and makes you less available to God so that you are free; and
- Spend time with God, because our joy (and the holiness of our lifestyle) is proportional to how available to God we are.

Forgive in Order to Be Joy-Full, A Key to Healing

Whether you've suffered grief, trauma, self-condemnation, or lesser offenses, forgiveness is a prerequisite to being free and full of joy. Without forgiveness, you cannot enjoy the freedom Christ died to give you, so let's examine what forgiveness is and isn't and how you know what or who needs forgiveness. Because forgiveness presents everyone with challenges, you should consider all its benefits.

Forgiving is a decision, an action, rather than a feeling. When it's hardest to do, it's an act of surrender to the power of God, because what's impossible for humans is possible with God's help.

Forgiving doesn't mean condoning wrongs or returning to abusive relationships, and it's not the same as reconciling with the other person. Forgiveness is also not forgetting, excusing, denying, or minimizing a hurt, stuffing your feelings, lowering your defenses, or getting an apology. Rather, it's more about coming to understand, however intentional an act that harmed or orphaned you was, the person probably didn't fully understand the damage they were doing to you.

Perhaps they weren't thinking clearly. For example, it occurred to me later that my husband's boss Joe, who threatened to kill anyone who questioned his leadership, may actually have been suffering from PTSD, because he mentioned his war experiences in the same breath. PTSD can seriously shut down rational thought when someone is triggered.

Forgiveness is your decision to give up your right to hold onto the offense. God will help you execute that decision.

A powerful inspiration to forgive is Jesus on the cross with His outstretched arms, saying, "Father, forgive them, for they do not know what they are doing" (Luke 23:34). Indeed, Jesus gave His life for the forgiveness of all our sins! So, to be like Christ, we must learn how to forgive and do it over and over until it's done. Remember Peter asking Jesus how many times he had to forgive a brother who sinned against him? Jesus told him to forgive others "seventy times seven times," which means until forgiveness is complete (Matthew 18:21–22 NLT, AMP, DRB).

Jesus also had to reassure a distressed Peter that he was still the one selected to shepherd the church, even after Peter had publicly denied Jesus three times. Jesus didn't hold the denial against him (*see* John 21:15–19).

Forgiveness is of crucial importance. In the Lord's prayer, Jesus taught us to make this alarming request: "Forgive us our debts as we also have forgiven our debtors" (Matthew 6:12). There can be no doubt about how critical forgiveness is when you consider this teaching of Jesus: "For if you forgive other people when they sin against you, your heavenly Father will also forgive you. But if you do not forgive others their sins, your Father will not forgive your sins" (Matthew 6:14–15).

We must also learn from the parable of the unmerciful servant, which shows that unforgiveness subjects us to torment emotionally, spiritually, and sometimes physically or financially. In Matthew 18, a king cancels a servant's debt of ten thousand bags of gold. Then that servant refuses to forgive a fellow servant's much smaller debt, a hundred silver coins. When told about it by observers, the king asked, "Shouldn't you have had mercy on your fellow servant just as I had on you?" The king then sent the unmerciful man to prison to be tortured. And Jesus said, "This is how my heavenly Father will treat each of you unless you forgive your brother or sister *from your heart*" (Matthew 18:32–35, NIV and NLT).

The last three words in that passage should alarm us if we hold onto grudges, desires for vengeance, or unforgiveness. "From the heart" means we can't just say, "I forgive" and count it done. This is why the British author and theologian C.S. Lewis says, "Everyone says that forgiveness is a lovely idea until they have something to forgive."[56] We must remember that only God can change hearts for good, as David stated in Psalm 51.

In his second letter to the Corinthians, the apostle Paul points out that unforgiveness gives the evil one an advantage in this life, so Paul urges people to forgive "in order that Satan should not outwit us. For we are not aware of his schemes," which include deception, lies, and blinding the mind of unbelievers, so they cannot see the light of the Gospel (2 Corinthians 2:10–11; 2 Corinthians 4:4).

---

[56] C.S. Lewis, *Mere Christianity (1952), page 115.*

Saint Paul called our spiritual adversary the "god of this age" (*id*.). Deceptions surrounding forgiveness keep the deceived person at risk of not forgiving, and not being forgiven—not only by God but also by other people, because of the biblical principle of correspondence: for the measure with which you measure will be measured out to you (Matthew 7:1-2).

The obstacles to forgiveness are many, including false notions of what forgiveness is. Three widespread obstacles are: not wanting to forgive a major hurt that the other person does not acknowledge; thinking forgiveness was complete when just mouthing the words didn't get to the heart of it; and not realizing that the person you need to forgive is yourself.

The mechanics of forgiving vary. I've learned from many excellent teachers and books, and best of all, from my own experiences, ranging from partial forgiveness initially to complete forgiveness later.

The benefits of forgiveness are amazing! You're improving your well-being and healing when you defeat the temptation to hold onto unforgiveness. You are taking responsibility for how you feel, taking back your power and authority. You gain peace and understanding and no longer let the past rule your present life. You're removing a block to experiencing God's love. You close the door to bitterness and resentment while opening the door to freedom, joy, peace, and greater closeness to God.

With a new heart, you may reconcile with the other person and resume love and connection by moving forward and operating out of choice, values, and sacred calling. Compulsion, poor habits, and obligation are no longer in control of you.

Empowering Seasoned Women to Rejoice Always and Let Our Light Shine

Yielding to God's plan and your calling is the surest way to joy. It's important to please God rather than conform to worldly norms and others' expectations. Most Christians, especially seasoned believers, have been faithful to God in small matters for years!

Many of us have focused on pleasing God by teaching our children to pray and raising them with Christian values at home. We've learned how to obey at least the letter of the Ten Commandments.

(The Beatitudes often present more of a challenge.) We may have taught Sunday school, led a women's group, volunteered at church, or served in a ministry or in other charitable organizations.

Most women have lovingly served immediate family members, older parents, adult offspring, their children's children or even their great-grandchildren. We might have found ways to serve God through business or through creative expression. And we probably made ourselves available for God to use for the sake of others, perhaps as witnesses to His marvelous works.

Yet, we may have disregarded the instructions not to serve by our own strength and understanding, but only with God's strength, wisdom, and gifts. Even so, there is still Good News. As we hear in the Parable of the Talents, the master said, "Since you have been faithful in small matters, come, share your master's joy" (Matthew 25:14-30 NAB). We can be like the workers who came to the vineyard to work in the final hour but still got the full reward (*id*.).

The biggest opposer to God is the self-embellished ego. Saul, who became Saint Paul, the great apostle to the Gentiles, had to let go of that. Paul's transformation and writings show that God wants to change the interior life so that every motive and action would be out of obedience and the desire to glorify the Lord, whom we love. Human nature often boasts about what we've done or want to accomplish. But those who know Jesus are being transformed by grace to glorify God through selfless service and unconditional love.

Jesus' prayer to the Father in John 17:13-19 (ESV) is for us and this process.

> "But now I am coming to you, [Father,] and these things I speak in the world, that they may have my joy fulfilled in themselves. I have given them your word, and the world has hated them because they are not of the world, just as I am not of the world. I do not ask that you take them out of the world, but that you keep them from the evil one. They are not of the world, just as I am not of the world. Sanctify them in the truth; your word is truth. As you sent me into the world, so I have sent them into the world. And for their sake I consecrate myself, that they also may be sanctified in truth."

Three Stories of Yielding to God's Plan and Experiencing Great Joy

In these examples, I refer to God's plan as taught by my denomination (Roman Catholic), but if you're of a different denomination, I believe the examples still bear witness to God having His way with us, communicating His desires, and rewarding an obedient listener with joy.

Joy and Baptism in the Holy Spirit. First, the story I told in Chapter One: I listened to the voice of a friend, urging me on God's behalf, to return to my faith after years of agnosticism and distance from the Church, failing to worship Jesus even after I recognized the role of the Creator in the birth of our first child. I did what my friend asked of me: I went to confession and Mass. To my surprise, I experienced sorrow for my sins, true repentance, and an about-face ("metanoia," a change of mind leading to a change of heart and drastically changed actions) following a previously unheard-of-by-me experience of baptism in the Holy Spirit. That day, my whole life began to center on the Holy Trinity, and my joy was astounding.

<u>Joy and Transubstantiation.</u>[57] Second, on
April 7, 2019, my husband and I were on a cruise that
ended in Buenos Aires, Argentina. A friend had put
me in touch with a priest in that city who had
witnessed an extraordinarily empirical Eucharistic
miracle that had not yet been officially approved.

I invited him to lunch at our hotel. Father Eduardo
Perez dal Lago arrived with a briefcase full of the
history and documentation of the testing of a
consecrated host. He told me it had been
desecrated on a candle holder in the back of the
church on August 18, 1996, in the Church of Santa
Maria y Caballito Almagro in Buenos Aires. Following
protocol, one of the priests placed the host in a
small bowl of holy water to dissolve, securing it in
the tabernacle (the ordinary practice for respectfully
handling such a host).

---

[57] See Magis Center, The Eucharistic Miracle Pope Francis
Witnessed in Buenos Aires, April 19, 2024,
https://www.magiscenter.com/blog/the-eucharistic-miracle-
pope-francis, accessed October 3, 2024 .There are a number
of accounts of the investigation of the story I'm about to tell,
other than my personal experiences of being with a priest who
was at the parish when these things took place, and with whom
my husband and I met in 2019. To read more about it, Google
it! And I used for reference the cited online article.

Based on the words of Christ in the Gospel of John, the Catholic Church professes that a consecrated host becomes the body, blood, soul, and divinity of Jesus.

> "So Jesus said to them, "Truly, truly, I say to you, unless you eat the flesh of the Son of Man and drink his blood, you have no life in you. Whoever feeds on my flesh and drinks my blood has eternal life, and I will raise him up on the last day. For my flesh is true food, and my blood is true drink. Whoever feeds on my flesh and drinks my blood abides in me, and I in him. As the living Father sent me, and I live because of the Father, so whoever feeds on me, he also will live because of me. This is the bread that came down from heaven, not like the bread the fathers ate, and died. Whoever feeds on this bread will live forever." ~John 6:53-58 ESV.

Father Eduardo then recounted the following sequence of events. Eight days after being placed in water inside the tabernacle, rather than dissolving as expected, the host looked like a piece of bloody tissue much larger than the original. Archbishop Bergoglio (now Pope Francis) asked to have the host professionally photographed and kept in the tabernacle without publicity. After three years, the bloody tissue had still not decomposed, even with no measures to preserve it.

Careful forensic testing ensued, including analysis by five scientists, including a famous cardiologist and forensic pathologist, Dr. Frederic Zugibe. When tissue samples were sent for testing, scientists and testing laboratories did not know the provenance of the tissue. The conclusions, which Father Eduardo showed us on the documents in his briefcase, were that the blood was type AB, from the left ventricle of a heart that had been wounded, with white blood cells indicating it had been taken from a living person.

You can find more details online. My husband and I saw the photographs and copies of the scientists' and doctors' reports. Father Eduardo told us that blood from the host had oozed onto a white linen cloth in his presence. Father Eduardo kept a piece of that linen with the blood on it in a small container called a reliquary. He let me hold it, and I kissed it and cried over holding the body and blood of Christ. At that moment, I truly experienced awe and wonder, the Isaiah 11:2-3 gift of fear of the Lord.

Suddenly, I realized that while I was witnessing evidence documenting a Eucharistic miracle, the same miracle happens at every Holy Mass when the substance of the bread is transubstantiated into Jesus' body, and the substance of the wine is transubstantiated into His blood.

Not only did I feel sorrow for my sins that Jesus had His heart pierced and gave His life for. I also had offended the Lord all the times when I had received communion without truly believing that I was holding Jesus' body and blood in my hands or on my tongue and consuming them. In tears, I confessed these sins and Father Eduardo gave me absolution at Sunday brunch in a beautiful modern restaurant.

Every time I am fed now by the Eucharist, this experience reminds me of the importance of honoring God, seeking His grace, and offering reverent awe for who God is. My prayer is for everyone to know what the Lord has done and continues to do for us, and to rejoice in the gifts, blessings, and promises He offers to those who love Him.

<u>Joy and the Last Rites</u>. Third, I was scheduled to attend four days at the School for Healing Prayer

in Albuquerque, New Mexico. I'd registered and paid for this SHP training months in advance. Missing the first of four levels would have required waiting another year and missing out on an important training opportunity at this stage in my life. The Monday morning it began, I learned that my 100-year-old mother (a full day of flying away from us) had fallen and hit her head. After being released from the Emergency Room, she had slept continuously and had been unresponsive for nearly a day. At her age, that certainly sounded as if the end was near. I prayed with the Monday morning SHP class, and I heard that the Lord would tell me when to get on a plane.

So, I waited, but first I called and arranged for a priest to visit my mom and give her the Anointing of the Sick (aka "Last Rites") that day. She made it through the week and the Lord had us fly on Saturday, but a massive snowstorm delayed our arrival, so we didn't see her until Sunday morning. Mom was alive when we finally arrived, but barely. However, over the next several days, she perked up and has since celebrated her 101st birthday, in better condition now than she was months earlier.

I thank God for the joy of my completing the School for Healing Prayer program and seeing my parents afterward, for directing me, and for the graces of the anointing, which also blessed my father. Mom and Dad have celebrated their 77th wedding anniversary and are still in love after all those years!

An added blessing was celebrating my 75th birthday with my Mom and Dad via Zoom, not only to my delight but theirs as well as the joy of friends and family who've known them for decades. Even those who were meeting them for the first time enjoyed seeing and hearing them participate in the online party. Faith, love of God and neighbors, and the joy of the Lord seem to have been the secrets to my mother's longevity!

PRAYER

*Most gracious Holy Trinity, thank You for being with me as I read this book and received words You wanted me to hear and take to heart. Please guide me to love and remain attached to Jesus: knowing, loving, and serving Him as He asks and desires. Jesus, remind me to stay yoked to You, with **abiding** love and trust! Your yoke upon me is also a call into the Word. In Your Holy Name, Jesus, I declare that there is no justification for hurry, worry, fear, hopelessness, or bearing burdens all alone. Help me, Lord, to **rejoice** always, to have a grateful heart, and to talk and listen to You throughout my days. Help me to be all that I can be, my REAL (free) self, with appreciation for the gifts You've given me to steward and even the crosses I bear with surprising fruit of the Spirit—with whom I walk, filled to overflowing and **aglow** with joy.*

REFLECTION QUESTIONS
(For Individual Use or with a Small Group)

1. Have any gifts or talents you stewarded well in your earlier life developed into greater talent, gifts, or resources over the years? How might God be leading you to use your gifts, talents, skills, or abilities now to bear good fruit?

2. Unforgiveness can block joy and the ability to be forgiven, healed, or set free. Deciding to forgive is the most important step in healing or Inner Work. Ask the Holy Spirit to reveal any areas of unforgiveness and note them. Also decide whether to seek help from a prayer ministry.

3. Write down the questions that keep popping up about any aspect of your life. Then pray for God to be with you and inform you, direct you, or provide clarification. In an undisturbed spot, handwrite each question, one at a time, then set a timer for ten minutes, and start writing out the answer that comes to you. Then move on to the next, and the next. Alternatively, use a method like the

4 Keys to Hearing God's Voice to bring each issue to God for Him to guide you into forgiveness and healing.

4. What are your biggest takeaways from this study of Joy or from the attention to second-half-of-life issues? What will you do differently as a result?

Conclusion

After reading this book and taking in its precepts, if you haven't done so already, I hope you'll make Jesus the center of your life and enjoy blessed intimacy with God, which looks something like this:

- Your relationship with Jesus will be based on knowing not just about Him, but rather, knowing Him through personal encounters and two-way conversations.

- You will seek the Lord's input when you're making choices, and you'll come to realize that's not out of a duty but because you are a friend of Jesus. You know He has perfect understanding and strategies, and He has ways of getting things done you can't even imagine, so it's your natural inclination to seek the Holy Trinity's, guidance, and direction—and you'll also receive Joy of the

Lord, which can be not only your strength but your Superpower!

When I set out to write this year, the Spirit of the Lord gave me the acronym FREEDOM. Although I didn't use that as an outline, I believe this is what we have covered:

F=Freedom in Christ (The Truth sets us free.)

R=Reprogramming (Forgiving, healing, and doing inner work transform the mind.)

E=Enjoy (Enjoy the process, enjoy the present, and leave the results to God.)

E=Especially in the second half of life (Yes!)

D=Delight (God's and ours!)

O=Obedience (Align and abide with God's command to love! Trust & surrender.)

M=Masterpiece with a calling (That's who you are!)

My prayer is that you found some profound nuggets causing you:

- to wonder,
- to notice,
- to choose to live with joy, and
- to share it with others,

- that their joy may be complete,
- that your joy may be complete, and
- that there may be more tastes of heaven on earth.
- I also pray that you will be filled with faith so that you know without a doubt that your prayers are heard and will be answered in the best possible ways and time. You'll trust God implicitly and surrender, which erases fear, anxiety, nervousness, worry, heavy burdens, and dread. You believe that greater is He who is in you than the evil one who is in the world seeking to keep you from intimacy with Jesus, from influencing others to yoke themselves to Jesus, and from eternal life. You'll see Christ in everyone and imagine the infinite love and joy of the Great Creator as your heart makes loving choices in all you do.

May God bless you abundantly to bear good fruit as you spread the love of the Holy Trinity and radiate the joy of the Gospel to the hearts of every person you encounter. Thank you for joining me!

Christine Boersma Smith

I encourage

RADIANT JOY

The 21-Day Joy Challenge

You might like to encourage yourself to live joyfully through the 21-Day Joy Challenge email series offered periodically through my website, *www.RadiantJoy.us/Joy-book*, or by short daily devotional readings in my devotional-style book, *The Radiant Joy Challenge: 21 Days to More Joy, Greater Peace, and New Intimacy with God*.

References

Chapter 1

1. Gem Fadling, Why Happiness ISN'T the Ultimate Goal, www.unhurriedliving.com, published August 14, 2024, accessed October 2, 2024, https://www.unhurriedliving.com/blog/why-happiness-isnt-the-ultimate-goal.

Chapter 2

2. Bishop Robert Barron, The Word on Fire Ministries, October 1, 2024, https://www.facebook.com/BishopRobertBarron/posts/1087821459368830/?paipv=0&eav=Afb8Y-NUacTfIhgbqmp65NSZqrv1CBy4l2ViljUxyMqmmPyfz6RFxyipWgqws_SEWSM&_rdr, accessed October 2, 2024 (emphasis added) (noting that "the best introduction to Thérèse's spirituality is a text that she wrote at the behest of Sr. Marie of the Sacred Heart, a sort of memoir of the retreat that she

made in September 1896, just a year before her death.")

3. Pam Wasserman, Population Education, "World Population by Religion: A Global Tapestry of Faith, PopEd Blog, January 12, 2024, https://populationeducation.org/world-population-by-religion-a-global-tapestry-of-faith/, accessed October 7, 2024.

4. Decline of Christianity in the Western world. (2024, September 18). In *Wikipedia*. https://en.wikipedia.org/wiki/Decline_of_Christianity_in_the_Western_world, accessed October 7, 2024.

5. Matt Lozano, *Free to Be Holy*, 2023, The Word Among Us Press, Frederick, MD, page 27 (Jesus' sacrifice makes us holy and we can't try to be holy apart from Him).

6. See Luke 17:21, 18:16-17 (NIV and DRB); Psalm 82:6; 1 Thessalonians 3:9; Acts 7:46; Luke 18:16; John 14:6; Acts 14:27; Psalm 47:8.

7. Katie Kindelan, Erin Brady, Zoe Magee, Adriana Pratt, Taylor Behrendt-Rhodes, Cleopatra Andreadis and Kate Hodgson, abcNEWS, ROYAL FAMILY, "Prince Harry opens up about rift with royal family and whether he can return to royal role: Prince Harry speaks to 'Good Morning America's Michael Strahan about his new memoir 'Spare,'" January 9, 2023, https://abcnews.go.com/GMA/Culture/prince-harry-opens-rift-royal-family-return-royal/story?id=96242779; Jennifer Clarke, BBC News, "Why did Harry and Meghan leave the Royal Family, and where do they get their money?" September 24, 2024, www.bbc.com/news/explainers-51047186, accessed October 27, 2024. Prince Harry also attributed his decision to fight against intrusion from the tabloid press as central to the breakdown of his relationship with the rest of the Royal Family. They had suffered from phone-hacking intrusions as well as incorrect tabloid stories about Meghan that Harry says palace officials failed to correct. Alex Smith, BBC News, "Press battle 'central' to Royal Family rift - Harry," July 24, 2024, www.bbc.com/news/articles/c6p2e3p5gr2o,

accessed October 27, 2024. In December 2023 a High Court judge ruled that Mirror Group Newspapers (MGN) had unlawfully gathered information for stories published about Prince Harry, who has since been awarded hundreds of thousands of pounds in damages.

8. 1 Corinthians 3:9, 1 Thessalonians 3:2; Colossians 1:24, 4:11.

9. Matthew 19:25-26; John 15:6; 14:13.

Chapter 3

10. Ryan Ermey, "Only 11% of American workers don't plan to work at all after they retire," September 6, 2024, MakeIt, LinkedIn, accessed September 6, 2024.

11. *Id. citing* Spencer Look, associate director of retirement studies at Morningstar Retirement.

12. Biography, Padre Pio Foundation of America, https://padrepio.com/padre-pio/biography/, accessed October 17, 2024

13. The Surrender Novena | Padre Pio Ministry to the Suffering, https://padrepioministry.org/surrender-novena/, accessed October 17, 2024

14. *Id.*

15. Second and Third John is estimated to have been written about a half-century after Jesus's death, when the Church had made a lot of progress but still faced a multitude of problems, leading one commentator claims that they demonstrate the apostle John's love for his audiences. (See "Second & Third John, Gaius, eyewitnessbible.org/other-letters/https://eyewitnessbible.org/other-letters/second-third-john/, accessed September 27, 2024).

16. See Wikipedia, Hildegard of Bingen, https://en.wikipedia.org/wiki/Hildegard_of_Bingen, accessed October 6, 2024.

17. Catholic Online, Saints & Angels, Saint Teresa of Calcutta,

https://www.catholic.org/saints/saint.php?saint_id=5611, accessed October 6, 2024.

18. I wrote this from memory, but it was based on the Baltimore Catechism I, Lesson 01. On the End of Man, the prevalent Catholic catechism for preparing American children for First Communion and Confirmation in the fifties. See Classical Liberal Arts Academy, Classical Education for Modern Students + Authentic & Accredited, William C. Michael, O.P., 12/7/2021, https://classicalliberalarts.com/catholic-theology/baltimore-catechism/baltimore-catechism-i-lesson-01-on-the-end-of-man/, accessed September 30, 2024.

19. Goodreads, Martha Graham>Quotes>Quotable Quote, https://www.goodreads.com/quotes/680327-there-is-a-vitality-a-life-force-a-quickening-that, accessed September 30 2024.

20. See https://biblehub.com/amp/matthew/5.htm, accessed October 8, 2024; see also Lockman Foundation, AMPLIFIED BIBLE,

https://www.lockman.org/amplified/, accessed October 8, 2024, which states: "Without sacrificing accuracy, the goal of the Amplified Bible is to reveal any other clarifying meanings from the original languages that may be concealed by the traditional translation method. It uses synonyms and definitions to explain and expand the meaning of words in the text. It does this by placing amplification in parentheses, brackets, and after keywords. As a result, English readers can clearly and completely grasp the meaning as it was understood by the readers of the original languages."

Chapter 4

21. Bill Johnson, Facebook, July 27, 2015, https://www.facebook.com/BillJohnsonMinistries/photos/any-area-of-our-lives-for-which-we-have-no-hope-is-under-the-influence-of-a-lie-/, accessed October 10, 2024. Bill Johnson is Senior Leader at Bethel Church in Redding, California.

22. WordHippo App, info@wordhippo.com, "What is another word for rejoice," accessed September 4, 2024.

23. Author's personal conversation on July 31, 2024, with Debbie Jordan, author of *Journey through Grief.*

24. See Dr. Aziz Gazipura's Author Page on Amazon.com, https://www.amazon.com/stor Hisziz-Gazipura/author/B00D0U4AMQ, accessed October 6, 2024, and his books *Not Nice: Stop People Pleasing, Staying Silent, & Feeling Guilty—And Start Speaking Up Saying No, Asking Boldly, and Unapologetically Being Yourself (2017)* and *Less Nice, More You: Stop Hiding & Become the Most Bold, Authentic Version of You Now (2023).*

25. I learned these (and much more) from Debrena Jackson Gandy, who has been a model of spiritual poise through life's ups and downs. See www.milliondollarmentor.net.

26. The thoughts are based on 2 Corinthians 12:10, Ephesians 2:10, Philippians 4:13 (ESV), and 1 Corinthians 15:57 (ESV).

27. *See* Sr. Kathleen Hughes, RSCJ, *Give Us This Day*, August 3, 2024, Reflection, "Divine Respect"

28. *Id.*

29. Email from The Harvard Gazette to an email list, October 16, 2024, including an article by Christine Perkins, Harvard Law Today - Campus & Community, "Give yourself grace," October 3, 2024,

30. The event was sponsored by the Albuquerque Catholic Charismatic Center Unbound Team.

31. Neal Lozano, *UNBOUND: A Practical Guide to Deliverance*, 2003, 2010, Chosen Books (Baker Publishing Group, Grand Rapids, MI, page 57.

32. If you have dabbled in the occult, or if your family members were involved in it, occult influences need to be cast out even if the only dabbling was seemingly insignificant (such as reading horoscopes or playing with a Ouija board). That's because those activities and more intense occult involvement can be entryways for seeking knowledge from an ungodly source. Demonic

influence can come to a person in relationships with other people affected by it and it can be quite oppressive, but it can be broken!

33. See Ephesians 1:3, 2:10 NLT, Psalm 139:14 NASB, 2 Timothy 3:17, Psalm 82:6 NLT, 1 Peter 2:9 ESV.

34. See Genesis 1:27.

35. Maxwell Maltz, MD, FICS, Psycho-Cybernetics, updated and expanded, 2015, Tarcherperigee, an imprint of Penguin Random House LLC, Chapter One, "The Self-Image: Your Key to a Better Life," pages 1-15.

36. Sarah Pangburn, "As If Nothing Had Yet Been Done," RelevantChurch.cc, The Gathering 2017 Summer Devotional Series, https://relevantchurch.cc/as-if-nothing-had-yet-been-done/, accessed October 9, 2024. (In my opinion, this article and its C.S. Lewis quotes are amazingly provocative and well worth pondering, and her article has influenced this part of my writing.)

37. 27 Christian Quotes from C.S. Lewis, Great American Pure Flix INSIDER, https://www.pureflix.com/insider/27-christian-quotes-from-c.s.-lewis-youll-love, accessed October 9, 2024. The full quote is: "God cannot give us a happiness and peace apart from Himself, because it is not there. There is no such thing."

Chapter 5

38. Catechism of the Catholic Church, Ascension Edition, 2022 ("CCC"), ¶1263, ¶1265 citing 2 Corinthians 5:17, *cf.* Galatians 4:56, 2 Corinthian 6:15; 12:27, Romans 8:17, 1 Corinthians 6:19.

39. See Bette Helaine Singer Harrison, *What Is a Nice Jewish Girl Like* me *Doing in Doing in the Catholic Church? 2018, Chapter 13.*

40. Pope Benedict XVI, "Deus caritas est" (God is Love encyclical), 2005, introductory remarks, also delivered at the inaugural session of the Fifth General Conference of the Bishops of Latin America and the Caribbean in 2007 (CELAM), quoted in Catholic Digest, October 5, 2024,

https://www.catholicdigest.com/from-the-magazine/quiet-moment/being-christian-is-not-the-result-of-an-ethical-choice/, accessed October 5, 2024.

41. See *Unbound Ministry Guidebook: Helping Others Find Freedom in Christ* (2011, 2014) by Neal Lozano and Matthew Lozano.)

42. See, e.g., Office of Catholic Charismatic Renewal Services, Diocese of Rockford, Illinois, "What is a Life-In-the-Spirit Seminar," https://charismaticrenewal.rockforddiocese.org/frequently-asked-questions/what-is-a-life-in-the-spirit-seminar/, accessed October 6, 2024
Chapter 6

43. F. B. Meyer, Bible, Commentary, Dictionary, "Deuteronomy 6:1-19: HOW TO TREAT GOD'S WORDS," e-Sword X, Version 9.4 (40), © 2024, Rick Meyers.

44. Mark and Patti Virkler, *4 Keys to Hearing God's Voice,* Communion With God Ministries,

https://www.cwgministries.org/store/4-keys-hearing-gods-voice. *Continued in References at the back of the book. A handout based on a page taken from the book urges people to "Copy and share." It shows the following, "As exemplified in Habakkuk 2:1,2" and "Stated Briefly" in Mark & Patti Virkler's words:

Key 1: "I will stand at my guardpost" is briefly stated as "Quiet yourself in the Lord's presence;"

Key 2: "I will keep watch and see" is briefly stated as "Look for a vision as you pray. Fix your eyes on Jesus;"

Key 3: "What He will speak to me..." is briefly stated as "God's voice often comes as spontaneous thoughts;"

Key 4: "Then the Lord said, 'Record the vision...'" is briefly stated as "Write out the flow of thoughts and visions. Called two-way journaling."

45. Dr. Mark Virkler, "Would You Believe the 4 Keys Were Taught 400 Years Ago?" Communion With God blog, Dec. 20, 2022. This blog post cites Madame Jeanne Guyon, A Short and Easy Method of Prayer, circa 1600s, English translation. It includes a link to a free download of the 1600s

book as well as his course on the 4 Keys to Hearing God's Voice. https://www.cwgministries.org/blogs/would-you-believe-4-keys-were-taught-400-years-ago

46. Dr. Mark Virkler, "All Uses of 'Rhema' in the New Testament," Communion With God Ministries, https://www.cwgministries.org/all-uses-rhema-bible, accessed October 10, 2024, *citing* Vine's Expository Dictionary notes.

47. Stormie O'Martian, *Just Enough Light for the Step I'm On* (Eugene, OR: Harvest House Publishers, 1999).

48. ©1994 Integrity's Hosanna! Music (Admin. by Capitol CMG Publishing (Integrity Music, David C Cook)

49. ©1995 Mercy/Vineyard Publishing

50. *Cf.* Psalm 42:4 and 43:4; Ezra 6:16 and 22.

51. Psalms 28:7; 30:11; 67:4; 90:14; 18:8, 119:111; 20:5; 65:8; 126:2; 94:19; 71:23, 105:43; 51:8, 95:1.

52. Ken Boa, Sunday Morning Study "Quotes from C.S. Lewis," Reflections with Ken Boa, *quoting* C.S. Lewis, *The Great Divorce*, chapter 9, https://kenboa.org/sunday-morning-study/quotes-from-c-s-lewis/, accessed October 10, 2024.

Chapter 7

53. *See* Sevil Omer, World Vision, "2004 Indian Ocean earthquake and tsunami: Facts and FAQs," updated August 14, 2024, https://www.worldvision.org/disaster-relief-news-stories/2004-indian-ocean-earthquake-tsunami-facts, accessed October 9, 2024

54. Entomology Today, The Entomological Society of America, "Ants Can Withstand Pressure Up to 5,00 Times Their Own Body Weight," February 11, 2014, Research News, *citing Journal of Biomechanics,* https://entomologytoday.org/2014/02/11/ants-can-lift-up-to-5000-times-their-own-body-weight-new-study-suggests/, accessed October 6, 2024.

55. *See* www.StephanieRichter.com.

56. C.S. Lewis, *Mere Christianity (1952), page 115.*

57. See Magis Center, The Eucharistic Miracle Pope Francis Witnessed in Buenos Aires, April 19, 2024, https://www.magiscenter.com/blog/the-eucharistic-miracle-pope-francis, accessed October 3, 2024. There are a number of accounts of the investigation of the story I'm about to tell, other than my personal experiences of being with a priest who was at the parish when these things took place, and with whom my husband and I met in 2019. To read more about it, Google it! And I used for reference the cited online article.

Reap as You Sew

Spirit at Work in Quiltmaking

This isn't a pattern book for making the quilts pictured in it. Rather, it's a book about process and inspiration. Each chapter includes a variety of practical exercises and reflections to enhance the connections between spirituality and creativity, particularly expressed through quilt making but applicable to other creative undertakings—making it a workbook you could come back to over and over. Book clubs have enjoyed discussing it, and it lends itself very well to small quilt groups looking for a different kind of challenge. The book features work by Christian quilters and other spiritual quilters, and has also fascinated non-quilters; the principles of living a creative life shine throughout its 111 pages!

Get it here: *www.RadiantJoy.us/books*.

About the Author
Christine Boersma Smith

 Christine encourages Christian women in their second half of life to live with more inner joy, holy boldness, and fruitfulness so they may embrace the blessings, surprises, and challenges of this season of life with grace and confidence. She's a ray of sunshine for those navigating the fog and late afternoon of their lives.

A Benedictine-trained spiritual director and transformational coach with twelve years of experience in healing and cleansing prayer ministry, Christine's passion is to partner with the Holy Spirit and encourage seasoned women to connect with one another and share meaningfully in this special season of their lives. She loves to help transform lives to be more joyful and fruitful: aligned with God, being who we really are, with holy and loving hearts.

Her books include *Reap As You Sew: Spirit at Work in Quiltmaking* and two books in the Light Up Your Life Series: *The Radiant Joy Challenge: 21 Days to More Joy, Peace, and Godliness* and *Joy-Full Seasoned Women: A Guide to Bearing Good Fruit and Radiating Joy in Your Second Half.* Find out more about Christine at www.RadiantJoy.us.

Thank You!

Thank you so much for reading *Joy-Full Seasoned Women!* If you have enjoyed it or it has impacted you, I always welcome emails from readers. Would you bless me by leaving an honest review of this book on Goodreads or on the Amazon book page? Reviews are gold to authors! They help reach more readers and impact more lives.